Also by Rick Gillis

PROMOTE! Your Work Does Not Speak for Itself. You Do.

JOB! Search Optimized

LEVELING THE PAYING FIELD

A Groundbreaking Approach to Achieving Fair Pay

Introducing the QTNT® Personal Value Calculation System

LEVELING
the PAYING
FIELD

A Groundbreaking Approach
to Achieving Fair Pay

RICK GILLIS
FOREWORD BY ALANA M. HILL

Indigo River Publishing
3 West Garden Street, Ste. 718
Pensacola, FL 32502
www.indigoriverpublishing.com

Leveling the Paying Field: A Groundbreaking Approach to Achieving Fair Pay | Rick
Gillis, author
ISBN 978-1-950906-96-3 | LCCN 2021900824

Edited by Dianna Graveman and Regina Cornell
Cover and interior design by Emma Grace
Graphs by Trifox Creative

The Quotient | QTNT | fair pay | pay equality | equal pay for equal work | pay disparity
proper pay | accomplishment | advancement | business management | employee
engagement | performance assessment | performance appraisal | performance review
personal growth | promotion | employment | #QTNT | #ProperPay | #LevelPayingField

Special discounts are available on quantity purchases by corporations, associations, and
others.For details, contact the publisher at the address above. Orders by US trade book-
stores and wholesalers: please contact the publisher at the address above.

*With Indigo River Publishing, you can always expect great books, strong voices, and mean-
ingful messages. Most importantly, you'll always find . . . words worth reading.*

CONTENTS

WHAT THEY ARE SAYING
about *Leveling the Paying Field*

In *Leveling the Paying Field* author Rick Gillis has brought his lifetime of career management experience to solving one of the hardest aspects of compensation and negotiation: quantifying performance and value fairly and accurately, regardless of role or gender. Gillis provides a simple, repeatable formula as well as many examples that illustrate that quantifying value is not just for those whose work directly impacts revenue. His "quotient" will work for everyone, from secretaries to project managers to executives. A must for HR and hiring managers.

LISA GATES, Negotiation and Career Story Coach,
StoryHappensHere.com

Rick Gillis may have resolved the issue of pay disparity in the workplace. By embracing the concepts laid out in this book, no matter what you do, you could realistically change your pay and your reality. The legacy of *Leveling the Paying Field* could be to change the lives of generations yet to come.

KEITH WYCHE, C-Suite Executive, Speaker & Author of
Good is Not Enough & *Corner Office Rules*

Having people answer the question 'resulting in?' has been transformational for my entire organization as well as our customers. *Leveling the Paying Field* has completely reframed the way we look at both customer delivery as well as employee compensation. The idea that we are expected to deliver "quantifiable value" has enabled our team to measure their performance and has directly 'resulted in' us being able to identify our A players and maintain scorecards for each customer engagement.

MISTY MAYES, PMP, CLSS, CCMP, CEO Management Solutions

What is true in life is true in business: rarely will others see your value until you do. In *Leveling the Paying Field*, Rick Gillis walks you through the "simple but not easy" process of discovering your obvious, and hidden, contributions to your organization. You'll learn to calculate and articulate your impact in financial terms, so you have agency in getting the compensation you deserve. Don't wait for the outside world to notice your value and pay you fairly. Use Rick's QTNT technique to develop yourself into a confident, self-aware individual, armed with a succinct, factual value statement of your contributions.

CATHERINE L. CROSSLIN, CEO, Instar Performance,
a Culture & Leadership Consultancy

Connecting people to their true value in any enterprise (volunteer, not-for-profit, or multinational corporation) boosts engagement, self-worth, self-confidence, and self-respect. Leaders can effect genuine relationships and connectedness with absolute value. In *Leveling the Paying Field*, Rick nails the concept and sticks the landing.

ROD BRANCH, CHRO, Thought Leader, Author & Speaker

Leveling the Paying Field, by an insightful leader in the field, Rick Gillis, offers a groundbreaking formula for employees or contract workers to assess their value to employers. Rick, after deep research, has come up with a deceptively simple yet profound formula for employees to determine their true value at work. Trust me, this book and formula are about to reset the new gold standard in measurement for both employers and employees. Kudos, Rick, you've just changed the game!

CATHLEEN FILLMORE, CEO, SpeakersGold.com

Rick Gillis' *Leveling the Paying Field* is a must-read for any supervisor who wants to quantify performance; their own, or those they evaluate. Putting numbers to the value of any employee's performance is always a challenge, but Rick has created a simple, powerful formula with immediate applications for transforming how your workplace produces and evaluates value.

ROB PENNINGTON, Ph.D., Educational Psychologist,
DrRobSpeaks.com

One of the more innovative thinkers in career management, Rick Gillis has hit a homerun for employers, employees, and job-seekers with an innovative approach to quantifying a person's value in correlation to his or her salary. In *Leveling the Paying Field*, Gillis introduces the Quotient (QTNT) a deceptively simple, yet amazingly rich way of measuring a person's contributions and accomplishments. As a career-coach and job search guru, I have found much of Rick's work in this field to be exceptionally forward-thinking—and this book takes it to the next level. We like to stress quantifying accomplishments whenever a person is looking for a promotion, a raise or seeking a new job, but *Leveling the Paying Field* provides even more power to the equation by coming up with a formula that measures contribution against pay. Through a very detailed examination of the topic and some excellent and thorough client examples, Rick demonstrates how the QTNT can be used by workers in all fields and in some very complex situations. If you are looking to examine your value to your current employer—or showcase how much value you will bring to your next employer—you need to read this book and develop your QTNT.

RANDALL HANSEN, Ph.D. Empowering Educator & Marketer

FOREWORD

THERE ARE SEVERAL reasons why pay disparity issues happen in the US but one that continues to surface, especially for women, is our unwillingness to advocate for ourselves. While much is written in the areas of assertiveness and communication styles what has been missing from this conversation are the metrics to advocate for oneself. Career management and job search expert, Rick Gillis, now offers a ground-breaking, potentially life-changing concept that provides you with a methodology to define your worth in the language of business: how to measure your financial benefit to the organization.

In *Leveling the Paying Field*, Rick provides a repeatable process for qualifying and quantifying an individual employee's contributions to their employer using a process he calls the Quotient. Not only do I wish this information had been available to me during my IT and HR project management career, it is an approach I would have used with my team. The Quotient, in its simplicity, gives rise to the ability to clearly state your value to your manager, to your company and, importantly, to yourself. When used in conjunction with the other accomplishment sourcing and valuation techniques Rick shares, you will learn a simple yet comprehensive way to confidently champion your worth.

You will be entertained by the 'Q-Studies'—actual stories of professionals Rick worked with—and see how their Quotient's were calculated step-by-step. *Leveling the Paying Field* is both anecdotal and academic giving you a rich understanding of how to apply the Quotient to your own career—today.

Rick Gillis challenges his readers to look at pay disparity as a problem you are able to overcome. That said, while Rick is bold in his approach, he's not naïve in his observations of the workplace. From chronicling personal success to negotiating salaries, this book will help you throughout your career. Especially those of you intent on achieving equal pay—or better.

As indispensable as the secrets in this book are to employees, they are equally valuable to the organization. How much easier is it to manage an employee who can clearly communicate their value? How much easier is it to aggregate the accomplishments of your team if each individual knows how to identify and share their successes? When your team is equipped with the tools that *Leveling the Paying Field* offers, they will be able to better describe their contributions and, in turn, be more empowered and engaged.

Having consulted with many companies in several industries, I can say for certain that the techniques in this book are valuable to employees and to those who lead them. When you can help your boss understand your contributions in an objective way everyone wins! Whether you are just starting out or seeking your next promotion, Rick has crafted the premier self-advocacy 'handbook' to help you compete not just for equal pay, but as Rick says, for the proper pay for the best performance.

ALANA M. HILL, PMP, Speaker, Author, Consultant
TheMsEngineerWay.com

INTRODUCTION

WHEN I WAS SIXTEEN, I held a part-time job that paid me $60 per week—oftentimes more. At the same time, my single mom, who was caring for my younger brother and me while working full-time, was earning $50 per week. I knew this was not right, but at that age and at that time, I didn't *really* understand why.

Looking back, from that part-time job to today, I now see that virtually everything I have done over the course of my life, every experience, good or bad, and nearly every job I have ever held, has been pivotal in bringing me to this place, to write this book and to invent a personal measurement process that I call the Quotient. I don't know that I would have recognized the Quotient for what it was had the idea come to me sooner.

A large part of *Leveling the Paying Field* is about pay parity—which I absolutely believe in—but it's about much more than that. My Quotient process—or more specifically, the QTNT® Personal Value Calculation (PVC) process (sometimes referred to as simply "the process," "the calculation," or "the contribution")—is a brand-new performance measurement tool designed for both the individual employee and the company.

In these pages I will show you how to achieve your best pay and how to confidently share your on-the-job contributions with management. I understand this may sound outrageous, but it's not. I stand by these statements. I have been using this process in my work with job-search and promotion-seeking clients with great success for more than fifteen years.

Contrary to traditional thinking, the QTNT PVC process, by design, puts you in charge of identifying and calculating your value regardless of what you do. I will show you how to professionally take the initiative at your performance review. This, too, may sound revolutionary, but— oh, wait—it is! There may be specific protocols for formal performance assessment within your company, but there are no rules when it comes to advocating for yourself—on the job, during your appraisal, or when seeking new opportunities. Importantly, none of this is difficult. There is nothing in this book that the motivated employee or manager won't understand.

To help you, I have placed fourteen entertaining, step-by-step, re-al-client accomplishment-measuring examples, which I call Q-Studies, throughout the book. The people in these stories, each of them, had done exceptional work but did not recognize the value they had delivered to their employers until we did a deep dive into their on-the-job achievements. What they learned was eye-opening. This does not mean their employers took advantage of them. On the contrary, as you will see in chapter 9, "Your Employer Is Not Responsible for Pointing Out Your Wins," it was up to them to figure it out. As it is for you.

The ideas in this book are big. They will impact many people and, by extension, many organizations, big and small, for the better.

Finally, *Leveling the Paying Field* was written for both the individual employee and those organizations who want to implement QTNT calculation ideas at their company. The enterprise chapters in the back of the book are the culmination of all that precedes them.

Welcome to *Leveling the Paying Field*.

RICK GILLIS

*The competition is continuous—and fierce.
It's called employment.*

—RICK GILLIS

1

The Quotient:
A Very Simple Idea

A CEO IS ASKED how many people work for him and he says, "About half." If this joke is funny to you, you probably don't manage people. The problem, universal to all owners and managers, is, Which half is doing the work? The answer to this question is not always as clear as one may think, especially when considering the many layers of management an organization may sustain. *Leveling the Paying Field* will sort all of this out for you.

* * *

To be competitive, a company must hire the best people available and pay them well in anticipation of getting the most value it can from each worker. The next hurdle is to be able to objectively measure every employee's performance to ensure the company is getting what it is paying for.

What if a company, with an employee's active engagement, is able to determine, based largely on a single metric, that a certain hire will likely be more successful than another person?

The Quotient Personal Value Calculation (QTNT PVC[1]) system can do this.

Employees, on the other hand, are rightfully seeking the highest-possible pay rate for their skills. What if an employee knows going in that she will be paid at the top of the pay scale? This is about more than equal pay for equal work. This is about proper pay for outstanding performance.

The Quotient can do this.

---

1   Based on context, you will find that PVC will also represent *Personal Value Contribution*. See QTNT PVC in glossary.

The QTNT process is about workers taking responsibility for their own pay and well-being; it is about a new kind of performance review. It is also about workers educating themselves on how, as well as how much, they contribute to their companies.

The Quotient is about employers embracing a new kind of compensation model based on their employees presenting their value to the organization in a defensible and reasonable manner. It is about employees performing as if they have some skin in the game—because they quickly learn they do.

The QTNT calculation is a metric so remarkably simple that, as you learn more, you will wonder why this measurement has never been used in business before now.

PERFORMANCE APPRAISAL

The Quotient, as designed, outperforms *subjective* performance-appraisal management systems, if for no other reason than current systems *are* subjective. The QTNT PVC process, in concert with the appraisal system I will introduce later in the book, helps employees set realistic, attainable goals and allows them, with management input and guidance, to manage the process on their own. How much time and money would that save enterprise? Millions? Billions? The *objective* QTNT calculation process can achieve this and more.

The Quotient has the power and the clout to positively impact all workers at all stages of their employment life cycle. And there's a bonus (sound the horns!): it's engaging and motivates employees to think like owners!

* * *

You may think that personal accomplishment is relatively easy to measure. Well, it is—if you are in sales—and it isn't if you are everybody else. Most employees don't have a clue how to measure the value of what they do.

To some, performance can mean as little as doing just enough to keep their job, or it can mean strategically outmaneuvering and outperforming the competition—their coworkers—enough to impress the powers that be and convince them that they are the person most worthy of promotion.

Keep all of this in mind as I share the Quotient with you. This powerful equation is simple and straightforward, but it is a management tool that will revolutionize how you prove your worth to your employer, how your employer will compare achievements among "equals," and how your division or branch will prove its value to the organization.

THE FORMULA

Before we go any further, let me share the Quotient formula with you:

CONTRIBUTION (C) ÷ Base PAY (P) = The QTNT Score

Where CONTRIBUTION equals the value of a worker's performance on the job divided by that person's rate of base PAY.

Never before has anyone divided a non-sales professional's personal value contribution to the company by his or her *rate of pay*. Why has this idea not been part of the business lingo before now? Probably because no one has ever thought to teach non-sales workers how to determine the value of their work before.

As a result of using this equation, employees can literally begin to take charge of their careers in a way that salespeople always have. The Quotient enables workers to determine their real worth to the company and to themselves.

Let's say, for example, that no one noticed when Ron came up with a little "tweak" in the IT security platform that saved the company $100,000 in reduced service calls. (These kinds of "little" savings occur in business all the time.) But Ron did. By calculating his Quotient for this event, he can capture the value of his contribution and, to his benefit, share it with his managers.

From the employee's point of view (and everyone, even the CEO, is an employee), what's important is that the employee learns how to identify those costs associated with what he or she does at work. A lot of the information in this book is devoted to helping you determine the costs associated with your own job or developing supervisor-acceptable workarounds you will be able to utilize to establish a value for what you do. These are the kinds of value *not* captured by your company's accounting systems.

Once you have this information, all you have to do is divide the total of the dollar value generated or saved by your rate of pay. The possibilities for the use and utility of the Quotient by you, by your employer, by big business, and even in the realm of big data and artificial intelligence are potentially astonishing.

In short, the Quotient separates the doers from the noisemakers—and makes our CEO happy to learn which half is getting the work done.

2 The QTNT Personal Value Calculation

I N MY PREVIOUS life, I was a job search expert. Over time, I became more of a "career therapist." I asked the questions necessary for my clients to observe the challenges they faced and to seek the creativity that led to their having accomplished all they did. I learned to identify achievements they might have overlooked. I guided my clients to look beyond the work they had done and focus on the specific *outcome* of that work as something *worthy of its own scrutiny*. I believe everyone should be able to assign a value to his or her own little piece of the puzzle.

The reality was that most of my highly knowledgeable and experienced clients were, except for a paycheck, often blind to the *actual value* of what they produced. For the most part, they just, well, went to work.

This is not unusual, and it's not bad. It's certainly more the norm than not. You do what you do. You do it well, day in and day out, and soon it just becomes what you do. What I eventually realized is that many people become so accustomed to simply putting in time on the job that they don't take the time to look around and think about how they can showcase their achievements. This requires an accomplishments mindset (more on this later) and attitude. And, as you will see over and over throughout the book, this is not about boasting.

PERSONAL ACCOMPLISHMENTS INVENTORY

I was involved with the first job board in the Houston, Texas, area, and the software, such as it was, at the time. Honestly, we were just making it all up!

I was mesmerized by the first applicant tracking systems (ATS) and résumé filtering software. I learned how résumés would be flagged and ranked by the terminology—the keywords—that matched those in the job postings. In those days, I was pooh-poohed by my audiences for insisting they utilize keywords on their résumés and in the online application. These days, it's impossible to believe that the concept was difficult to accept. The concepts I created back then are accepted job-search strategy today.

Once a client learned how to successfully navigate the ATS, the next step was to school them in how to share previous on-the-job accomplishments with a future employer. The real "secret sauce" that landed my clients their next position was my nonnegotiable insistence that they invest quality time in developing a Personal Accomplishments Inventory. This takes a little investigation and some introspection, but those who did it well became successful very quickly.

While what I'm describing here is contemporary job search, this concept is equally important for your "commercial" well-being on the job. Prove to someone how you can make them money or save them money, and you will always be in it—the money, that is!

EMPLOYING THE QUOTIENT

It was from this perspective that I came up with the QTNT PVC process and formula, and it is game-changing! Let me remind you of what the Quotient equation looks like, and then we'll look at some basic examples.

Contribution (C) ÷ Base Pay (P) = QTNT
Personal Value Calculation

Where the value of your CONTRIBUTION[2] on the job as determined by you or your employer is divided by your base, or gross, PAY.[3]

EXAMPLE 1

Let's say your base pay this year was $50,000. You and your supervisor mutually agree (by means that we will discuss later in the book) that you delivered $250,000 in value to your company during this period. Your Quotient calculation would look like this:

$$\frac{\text{The value of your Contribution (C)} = \$250,000}{\text{Amount of (base) Pay (P)} = \$50,000}$$

Your QTNT Score = 5, or 5 times your annual pay

---

2 You might prefer to use such terms as *deliverables* or *work product* instead of contribution.
3 Do not use net, or take-home, pay for this calculation.

This means the value you delivered to your company this year is five times greater than your annual pay. Most likely, you are making money for your company.

EXAMPLE 2

$$\frac{\text{Contribution} = \$1,500,000}{\text{Pay} = \$50,000}$$

**This employee's QTNT contribution = 30,
or 30 times their annual pay**

The "**Rule of the Quotient**," as you can see, is the larger the Quotient (the result of a division calculation), the larger or more valuable the worker's contribution to the organization. In other words, the employee whose QTNT Personal Value Calculation/Contribution (PVC) equals 30 is more valuable to her company than someone who scored an 18 or a 9. (Notice this definition also applies to teams, departments, branches, divisions, etc.)

AN INTRODUCTION TO THE Q-STUDIES

Before we move on to chapter 3, I want to share with you my first Quotient sample accomplishments calculation story. Strategically placed throughout the book are fourteen real-world former-client quantification examples for your consideration. These stories, or **Q-Studies** as I call them, are designed to compel you to think about what you do or have done on the job that is worthy of quantification. Besides being entertaining, these relatable, direct-from-my-files summaries show how I took client accomplishments and calculated their personal contributions on the job as well as the Quotient (QTNT score) for each. You will find these examples helpful as you begin recalling and calculating your own wins.

I encourage you to choose your favorite presentation style (as they vary somewhat) and think about using that format as a template for crafting your own personal accounts.

Vijay: Coder
"10,000 Lines of Code"

Vijay was testy. At one of my job search workshops, he told me that while completing a six-month project the previous year, he had written ten thousand lines of code and had been paid for his time. However, he had *no idea* how to establish a value for the work he had done. How the heck was he going to determine his Quotient?

I surprised him when I accepted his challenge and told him that I knew exactly where he was coming from. The fact is Vijay's predicament is common for those who do project, contract, or temp work—as well as those who have forgotten all the great things they have accomplished in the past. I told Vijay that all he had to do was reach out to the person who had supervised him. This person would have had to justify the money that was spent on his contract.

The thought had never occurred to Vijay that even though he was "just a contractor" (his words, not mine), someone inside the company would have been responsible for his work product. (Keep that in mind, contractors! Your good work could make somebody's career and get you the callback, or, conversely, your lousy work could kill somebody's career.)

SAVINGS AT THE ATMs

The customer for this project was a bank with multiple locations across Texas. The bank had hired Vijay to rewrite and implement the software responsible for the bank's automated teller machine (ATM) security and personal identification number (PIN) system. Vijay was paid $40 an hour for the work he did over a six-month period.

The first thing we must do here is to determine his total pay.

1040 hours (52 weeks x 40 hours ÷ 2) x $40 hour = $41,600 gross pay

When he caught up with his former supervisor, Vijay learned that he had done an outstanding job, which is always good to hear! In addition to having written and installed code that worked the first time, he had saved some *four hundred hours of monthly service calls* on the bank's ATMs across the state, a by-product no one had anticipated. This was a direct result of the bank having fewer problems with the machines and requiring less on-site attention after Vijay's code had been implemented.

Asked what those savings might amount to, the bank's IT manager had no idea. This may seem like a problem, but it really wasn't. Based on what he *did* know (four hundred hours saved), Vijay and I pulled a conservative value out of thin air for an ATM service attendant's cost to the bank per hour. (You can also search this kind of information online.) Let's guesstimate that the attendant costs the bank $100 an hour. We deliberately selected a low hourly rate, one that would not be challenged.

Just like Vijay, I encourage you to insert your own values as long as they are reasonable and would be accepted by an authority, such as, in this case, the bank's ATM manager. In the event you are uncertain what "reasonable" might look like, always go with the most conservative numbers so as not to exaggerate any values you claim. Remember: at some point, you may have to defend your calculations.

Here are some items that you might include in this valuation: one employee's rate of pay (we later learned that the bank's ATM service policy always required, at minimum, two people on-site) + training + travel/downtime + vehicle expense + equipment + phone and computer + administrative overhead + various insurance and business costs. When you add up all these factors, you can see that $100 is exceptionally conservative.

$100 per hour x 400 saved hours = $40,000 per month in savings

For our purposes, it's not out of line for Vijay to assume that his work will benefit the bank, at minimum, over the next twelve months. Because this was such a brief (six-month) contract, I recommended that he should calculate his personal value for this performance for one year from the time of completion.

$40,000 monthly savings x 12 months = $480,000 in savings annually

To determine Vijay's Quotient, all we need to do is divide the value of his contribution by his pay (C ÷ P = QTNT score).

$$\frac{\text{Total additional value delivered by Vijay} \;=\; \$480{,}000}{\text{Payment for ATM security project} \;=\; \$41{,}600}$$

Vijay's QTNT PVC for this project = 11.5

As you can see, this was an excellent use of the bank's funds with results that exceeded the cost of Vijay's service by more than eleven times. This unanticipated result was a bonus to both the bank and Vijay.

After doing this very simple math, Vijay was now able to pitch the result to other companies where he might seek work. He can even add this score to his résumé. As a result of his code-writing skills, he can now share how he was instrumental in saving a bank with multiple locations statewide some $500,000 annually, or eleven times what he was paid for his services.

Can you think of anything you've done lately that could be similarly quantified?

3 Three Kinds of QTNT Scores

THERE ARE THREE types of Quotient scores. The first, and most important, is a Quotient of 1 (indicated as Q = 1 or simply =1 and stated as "equals one"). This is a "perfect" Quotient. Note that I did not say this is an "ideal" Quotient; that would depend on the position or the kind of work being done and the expectations of the employer.

An employee who scores an =1 is doing exactly what he or she is supposed to be doing: nothing less, nothing more. Depending on the position, this is not a bad thing. Had Vijay, in the previous Q-Study, not reached out to the bank IT manager and learned he had saved the bank all those hours in reduced service calls, he would have, at best, only been able to claim an =1 for his good work on the security software.

Vijay aside, an =1 worker is the kind of worker who is necessary, vital, and valuable to every organization. A warehouse stocker who shows up on time and delivers a consistent effort is an example of just such a worker. This employee is delivering fair value to the organization in exchange for fair pay.

At the other end of the scale is the rock star who is brought on board to write code that will become the next big tech innovation. For this person to score an =1 would be considered a colossal failure.

The second type of Quotient, which you saw in examples 1 and 2 in chapter 2, is a quotient greater than 1 (indicated by Q > 1 or simply >1 and stated as "greater than one"). This happens when a worker delivers a work product greater than what was anticipated. A Quotient of 4 means you are delivering four times more than your base pay.

The last Quotient type is a quotient of less than 1 (indicated by Q < 1 or <1). This Quotient score speaks to a failure to produce at an adequate level for the company—except this might not always be the case. As you will see in the next chapter, "Three Ways of Looking at a $Q < 1$," there are talented, hardworking people who do not—and may never—achieve a Quotient of 1 or greater but who, nonetheless, bring tremendous value to their organization based on what they do.

THE QUOTIENT AND WEIGHTING

Companies may decide to establish an "ideal" or a minimum weighted Quotient for every position in the organization. The ideal Quotient for each position (do not confuse position with employee) can be weighted based on factors such as workforce availability, the skillset required, and the measurement of deliverables necessary for the position to be deemed successful as determined by the company.

Weighting may also refer to hiring when a predetermined or prenegotiated Quotient-based rate of return is expected by the organization in exchange for a specific compensation package.

Weighting will be discussed in greater detail in chapter 37.

4

Three Ways of
Looking at a Q < 1

THE LAST OF the three kinds of Quotient outcomes is the Q < 1, which has two different meanings *depending on the position* and the quality of the work being delivered. Stay with me here.

The first and most obvious way of looking at a Q < 1 pertains to the employee who is not meeting standards and, unless performance improves, will be let go. Let's explore other types of employees with a QTNT Personal Value Contribution score of less than 1.

HIGHLY VALUED EMPLOYEES WITH A QTNT PVC SCORE OF LESS THAN 1

Termination is the last thing on the minds of employers for the next group of <1 employees. This <1 occurs due to tenure and is an expense accepted by all employers. I'm referring to some very important, talented, and qualified employees in your company who do a fantastic job. These people may be the glue that keeps your operation running smoothly—or at all. These are the workers who do consistent and reliable work but who, over the years, have received pay increases and when compared to the market no longer achieve a Q = 1. Importantly, they continue to do exactly what they were hired to do and do it well.

Positions such as accounts payable and accounts receivable clerks, administrative assistants, or warehouse workers will, naturally, be hired at current market rate. Assuming they survive their first year on the job, we can presume they have achieved a QTNT PVC score of 1. Further assuming they continue to perform at a level that warrants their being kept on the job and that they continue to do the same type of work, by all rights, they should never have a <1. But based on the QTNT PVC formula, this is not the case.

Over the next few years, as an AP clerk continues to receive merit-based and cost-of-living pay raises but remains in the same position doing the same work, his or her QTNT PVC may actually begin to diminish.

As raises accrue, the employer *could* go back out to the street and advertise for a new staff worker to fill that AP position at the *current* market rate, which would be less than the current employee is now earning after several years of raises. Of course, this is not going to happen. Over time, it is the norm that a staff employee will be earning more in a current position than if he or she went back out on the market. This employee, unless promoted, has a job description that limits marketability—e.g., "Performs routine accounting work."

What I'm saying is that, over time, the *market* rate for a quality staff employee may cost you less (in dollars) were you to replace them. But do you go out and replace a tried-and-true experienced employee just because you can get someone for less money? Not likely.

THE INVALUABLE EXECUTIVE ASSISTANT

What about the executive assistant (EA) to the CEO who is earning $120,000 per year after being with the company for twenty-one years? The current market rate for this position today would be in the range of $55,000 to $70,000. In this case, the employee is invaluable to the organization, and his or her salary reflects that. The EA was there before the current boss and may be there for the next. He or she represents continuity in the corporation and is both confidant and gatekeeper. The boss has never missed a meeting, an appointment, or a flight and is always on time, always prepared. The CEO achieves great things, which is in no small part due to the EA's performance.

HOW TO DEAL WITH A Q < 1

So what is the solution to an employee who is doing a great job, someone you would not want to lose, but who, due to comparative market rates and expenses, earns an annual Quotient of, say, a .7 or worse? The answer here is twofold. One solution is *weighting*—that is, the weighting of QTNT PVC scores for all positions in an organization. Another solution, which in some cases I like better, is to *exempt* those few specific employees from Quotient rating altogether.

Let's look a little closer at these options. The first would be to apply that .7 rank. In this case, it would be important that *future* supervisors are informed that this score is based NOT on lack of performance but rather on staying true to the QTNT process. I would be afraid this vital piece of information could get lost in the transition.

The next possible solution would be to designate some employees as Q1 employees and exempt from scoring. Exempting certain employees—that is, ranking them as =1 or QE (Quotient exempt)—would require that their performance and compensation be specially reviewed by the head of compensation or a committee so that specific value could be appraised and rewarded.

Lisa: Executive Assistant
"You might be surprised."

Lisa is an executive assistant to both the CEO and the COO at a midsize healthcare organization. She began with the company as an administrative assistant a little over eight years ago and had the talent to work herself up very quickly past the numerous assistants and supervisors who people such an organization.

One of Lisa's leading soft skills is being unafraid to professionally challenge someone in authority. This leadership skill is one of several that have served her well and propelled her past all other employees who may have had their eye on working in the C-suite.

SAVING $72,000 IN ONE DAY

Lisa and I were talking recently, and I asked her if there was anything she had done on the job lately that she was particularly proud of. Having heard some stories of my clients having saved their companies "millions of dollars," she said she had never done anything comparable. I responded, "You might be surprised."

I pressed her to *really* pay attention to what she actually *did* on a daily basis and to not just go through the motions. A couple of weeks later she called to tell me about some significant savings she had discovered for her company.

The company had a contract in place to manage electronic payments. A coworker was responsible for paying invoices and tracking those payments against a monthly minimum required by the agreement, but she had been missing something important.

Wisely, before reviewing her coworker's performance, Lisa took it upon herself to study the original agreement. What she learned was that, while the person in charge of the contract was worried about making minimums, the contract offered a discount when the organization hit a certain threshold each month. Lisa discovered that these discounts were not being applied and that her company was owed $72,000.

In a single day, Lisa was able to track down $72,000 in new money for her company. Not a lot of money, right? Wrong—because it's all relative!

CALCULATING LISA'S QTNT SCORE

Lisa identified an amount of money that was $6,000 more than the $66,000 she was earning at the time. In one day, she identified a savings equal to more than her annual rate of pay, and the cost to the company was only one day of pay, if that, while she was doing her "regular" work.

Note, too, that Lisa not only recovered money for the organization, but the company will continue to reap this benefit as a result of her efforts.

Let's look at how Lisa's discovering this credit for the company affects her annual QTNT PVC score. (Remember: saving money for your organization, for our purposes here, is the same as generating revenue.)

Since Lisa is the executive assistant to the CEO and the COO, we can assume she already warrants a $Q = 1$ for the quality of her work. All we have to do to determine her new PVC score is add her $66,000 salary to her newfound $72,000 in value and divide that by her base pay (the same $66,000).

$$\$66,000 + \$72,000 \text{ in personal value}$$
$$\text{contribution (PVC) to her company} = \$138,000$$

$$\frac{\$138,000 = \text{total value of contribution}}{\$66,000 = \text{annual salary}} = \text{a Quotient of 2.09}$$

In less than one eight-hour day, Lisa measurably doubled her value to her company—something she might not have recognized if she weren't knowledgeable about the Quotient concept and, more importantly, had not been paying attention to what she was doing. Makes you wonder what she will accomplish tomorrow, right?

So, no, Lisa did not have million-dollar accomplishments she could point to, but, as I told her, it is important she continue to take personal note of her daily and weekly wins so she can get credit for them in a merit-based pay raise or at least at bonus time. Let's face it, a few $72,000 deals here and a few $72,000 deals there—from someone who is not tasked with generating revenue—and pretty soon we're talking about some real money!

5 Salespeople Don't Need the QTNT Process—Yet

GOALS, QUOTA, PLAN—these are terms all salespeople live by daily. Sales professionals know the numbers that must be met in each sales period to keep their jobs. It really is that simple, but also really that hard. Starting each month at zero, even with a base, is why many people are so deathly afraid of selling as a career choice.

Candidly, if you are an active sales professional, you probably don't need the QTNT PVC at this point in your career. You are already in tune with the idea that if you don't go out and sell something this week, you may not be employed next week. Coworkers who live on a weekly paycheck—and are dependent on you—don't necessarily understand how the game works.

As a salesperson, you already have an accomplishments mindset. You inherently understand the fundamentals that make up the Quotient. It's just that no one has ever asked you to delineate the "quotient" part from the accomplishment, meaning you have probably never before divided your annual production by your end-of-year pay—base, commissions, and bonuses combined. But you can bet someone has. You know your management team understands exactly what kind of value you are delivering.

So why would I say you don't need the Quotient? Well, to be more accurate, you may not need it right now. But one day, not too long from now, you will need it, so you may as well get the basics down now.

For those of you who stay the course and remain in sales, many will become sales managers and district managers and so on. Those professional salespeople who continue to learn on the job while on their way to becoming senior management know they will have to learn to manage more than just the sales team.

A sales manager, given the responsibility, can expect to manage the entire staff involved in support of the sales function and the delivery of the product sold. From the warehouse to the front office, that's a lot of managing. As a VP of sales, you can also count on there being several branches and divisions that will require Quotient scoring and ranking.

Problems create opportunities.
Opportunities create accomplishments.

—RICK GILLIS

6 Your Work Does Not Speak for Itself

NOT SURPRISINGLY, EMPLOYEES rarely speak the same language as employers or managers—until they become one themselves. I am referring to the language of accomplishment and performance.

Something I find interesting—as only someone who does what I do could—is that once candidates become employees and start doing their jobs, seldom if ever do they talk or think about the ways their individual efforts contribute to the overall mission or stated goals of the company. They just become a part of "the team"—which, from an employer's point of view, is a good thing. While I support "the team" (nothing gets done without a team!), I strongly believe in an individual's need to express the value he or she personally brings to the table.

Even senior managers who are "in the loop" and "plugged in," and who offer well-thought-out guidance on the company's next big initiative, rarely if ever stop to consider how the job they do *individually* contributes to the overall prosperity of the organization. I know this to be true. I have counseled several of them.

Then there is the certainty that, no matter your position, your boss may take credit for the work you do. This is not necessarily a slight on you or your work, or even your boss, as I address in the next chapter. It is, however, reason enough for you always to have a quantifiable performance inventory at hand and the confidence to speak up for yourself on an as-needed basis, as well as on an "irregular-regular" basis when the opportunity presents itself. Let me offer you one of my time-tested mantras: *Your work does not speak for itself. You do.*

Before you speak about yourself, you have to know what you're going to say beyond the fact that you occupy a desk from eight to five, five days a week. There is nothing wrong—well, actually there is—with keeping a seat warm, but being on time does not garner the same attention (or the bonus or the promotion) as telling someone how you made a difference. How you impacted the company's mission. How you made the company money. How you saved a bunch of bucks. This is the kind of personal value information you should have at your fingertips at all times.

WHAT AND WOW!

Success is about What and Wow! (I'll be repeating this phrase through-out the book, so get used to it.) A narrow, dictionary-type definition of accomplishment is "something that has been done successfully." My definition of What and Wow! incorporates this elementary definition but goes a step further. What and Wow! consists of having successfully achieved something you are proud of and then taking the time to share that success with your coworker(s) or your immediate supervisor or that senior VP you occasionally ride up the elevator with.

"What" describes what you did (duh!), while "Wow" is what you will hear from someone as you share your success(es) with them.

"Wow!" is usually followed by "How did you do that?" Wow is a good thing. You will learn a lot about your Wows in this book, as well as how to successfully share them.

What? You're not comfortable sharing your wins? I'm not surprised. You wouldn't be the first person I have worked with who was uncomfortable with the idea of talking about themselves, but I expect I'll be changing your outlook as we navigate these pages together. Breathe in. Breathe out. I do not promote bragging. I do not condone boasting. On the contrary, I'm simply suggesting that appropriately sharing your personal wins could make all the difference between just being paid and being paid well. What this is about is informing others of your personal wins and explaining how the organization is also winning as a result. Bragging is bad. Informing is good. And appropriate. And professional.

7

It's OK for Your Boss to Take Credit for Your Work (Ouch!)

DON'T GROAN WHEN I say it is not out of line for your immediate supervisor to take credit for your work. In certain scenarios—cases where your supervisor reports to his or her superiors—this can be the natural order of things. You may not like it, but it is what it is. (Then there are the "land grabbers" who need to be dealt with. See Chapter 10, "You Are Responsible for Pointing Out Your Wins," for tips to defend yourself against a supervisor who blatantly takes credit for your work.)

Here's how it happens: Your boss will say to his boss, "I completed the update of the human resources policy manual." This is an accurate statement as it was his assignment to bring the manual current. What he failed to mention was the involvement of the three staff members (you and two others) who did the lion's share of the work.

Will your boss share your specific contribution to the overall win? Maybe, but probably not. There is generally no time allotted in senior staff meetings for mentioning all the people who broke their backs to get a project done on time, and there are no "scrolling credits" at the end of a status report. All your boss's boss wants to know is whether the job got done.

SHARING YOUR ACCOMPLISHMENTS

This is why it's essential that you begin to share your wins with your boss (or maybe skip your immediate supervisor, right?) as well as the corporate hierarchy up to and including the CEO (yes, the CEO!) whenever possible. (See "The Perfect Elevator (or Anywhere Else) Pitch" in chapter 11.)

Senior management came up the same ladder you are currently

climbing. And senior management truly does understand how all employees interact for the well-being of the organization. Remember, this is not bragging. This is informing. This is communicating your value in a highly professional, timely, and appropriate manner regardless of your rank or status on the job. Remember my mantra: *Your work does not speak for itself. You do!*

Is it inappropriate to talk to your boss's boss about your performance? No. Your boss's supervisor can hear in your voice whether you are on the attack or simply speaking up about something you are proud of. There is a big difference. If you are going for the dig, well, that's a different book.

The bottom line? Never expect your boss to speak up for your benefit. This is not to say your supervisor won't or doesn't. It's just smart to expect that you may be required to carry this ball across the goal line on your own. The QTNT PVC provides that opportunity.

Q-STUDY NO. 3

Paula: Executive Search
"What have I done?"

A good friend of mine, Paula, called to ask me for some advice on her résumé. This struck me as kind of peculiar because Paula is in the résumé business. She has had world-class success in the staffing and executive-recruiting field, which is based almost exclusively on accomplishment! I couldn't help but hear the old saying in my head "You can't see the forest for the trees." (There is a lot of Quotient-related truth in that statement.) More importantly, her story illustrates one of the overriding themes in this book, which is that people do not recognize the value of their own work—something they spend about a third of their lives doing!

When we spoke, Paula told me she had hoped her most recent position would be her last professional job. But the startup company she had been working with underbudgeted and overspent during their first couple of years in business. They cut everywhere they possibly could but had to shut down in the end. Paula found herself out on the street and looking for a new position.

She asked if I could review her résumé, and while we were talking, out of the blue, she astonished me by blurting out, "What have I done?"—with the emphasis on "I."

I have known Paula professionally for ten years or more, and I know what she has accomplished. But once again, here was a mindset surfacing that I have seen over and over throughout the years.

When I thought about it, this question was not about what Paula had done but more about the lack of acknowledgment she had received for her achievements. Paula was expressing her frustration over her lack of recognition for the contributions she made and the value she created for those companies she worked for so diligently. Yes, she had been paid well for her work, but an occasional slap on the back is always appreciated no matter the rank or the status of the employee.

Paula has worked for several Fortune 100 companies. She is in the verifiable-performance business. Nobody gets past Paula who can't prove his or her value. Knowing this, I challenged Paula to provide me with an approximate number of people she had staffed in any one of her previous positions. That's when I learned that in the twenty-plus years she has been in the business she has kept a written record of *every placement* she ever made, as well as each person's annual starting salary!

I asked if she would provide me with a starting salary *total* for all those people she had placed while working at all the various companies throughout her career. She didn't have this information on an electronic spreadsheet, so, instead of adding up twenty-plus years' worth of individual salaries, Paula did some perfectly acceptable averaging, which, as you will see below, suited my needs perfectly.

The rate of annual pay for her placements ranged anywhere from $52,000 to $170,000. After looking over the list of candidates she had landed during her most recent ten years, Paula determined that $85,000 was a reasonable *average* salary rate.

However, for Company A (see list below), where she spent her first twelve years in the staffing business, she determined that an average rate of $75,000 was more in line. Approximations and averages are OK to use in your calculations as long as they are conservative and appropriate.

Paula then provided me with the annual salary for each position. Below are the calculations I made to determine Paula's career-long PVC and her resulting Quotient.

Note: The companies (first column below, G–A) Paula worked for are listed in reverse order with her most recent (Company G) at the top. The number of placements and compensation listed is for a single year unless otherwise noted.

Placements x Salary = Revenue	Paula's Annual Compensation
G: 125 x $85,000 = $10,625,000	$253,000 (2 yrs.)
F: 30 x $85,000 = $2,550,000	$140,000
E: 85 x $85,000 = $7,225,000	$105,000
D: 200 x $85,000 = $17,000,000	$300,000 (3 yrs.)
C: 85 x $85,000 = $7,225,000	$100,000
B: 103 x $85,000 = $8,755,000	$190,000 (2 yrs.)
A: 1200 x $75,000 = $90,000,000	$1,311,000 (12 yrs.)
Revenue Total = $143,380,000	Total Compensation = $2,399,000

Across the staffing industry, an agency, on average, earns between 20 and 25% of the placement's first-year salary. Of course, this rate can fluctuate depending on the position and the industry, but in this case, and in the interest of not overvaluing Paula's accomplishments, we will use the lower commission rate of 20% in our calculations.

22 years of gross revenue = $143,380,000 x 20% = $28,676,000

This is the amount customer-companies paid to Paula's various employers for her work.

Total commissions paid to Paula's employers	**= $28,676,000**
Total compensation Paula was paid	**= $2,399,000**

Paula's career QTNT PVC score = 11.95

During her most recent job search, I asked Paula how many recruiters could walk into an interview and categorically state they had delivered on the order of twelve times more than they had earned in compensation from their employers over their careers and that they had been personally responsible for more than $28,000,000 in commissions to those employers?

PAULA'S IMMEASURABLE CONTRIBUTION CALCULATION

As you will recall, Paula was exceedingly frustrated when she first called. She had asked me the rhetorical question "What have I done?" —as in her entire life! In answering this question, the first thing I pointed out was the economic impact she had directly had on all those families who were able to buy houses and cars and send their kids to school in nice clothes because of her work. This is a big deal. Additionally, the butcher, the baker, and the candlestick maker also do well when one more person is working full-time and spending money in their shops. That's what Paula had done!

ONE LAST THOUGHT

In the event your company does not know about the Quotient, you can still use the type of calculations I just shared with you. You can demonstrate the value you deliver exactly the same way Paula did when she determined she had returned to her previous employers twelve times what she had been paid.

In Paula's next interview, she slid a copy of those figures across the conference room table and got the job.

Once candidates become employees, seldom, if ever, do they think about all the ways their efforts contribute to the overall mission.

—RICK GILLIS

8 Your Commercial Value

YOU WERE HIRED because someone believed you would produce more value for the organization than you would cost it. This is a very simple definition of your commercial value.

You have probably never considered your value to an employer in this manner before, but the fact remains that if an employer can find someone who does what you do as well as you do it and for less money, then your commercial value is not as high as you may think it is. The QTNT PVC process is the only tool available to you to calculate your commercial value for yourself as well as to share with your employer.

Every worker the world over has commercial value. It impacts where you work, how well you are paid, and how long you will be on the job. You remain valuable to a company, and, therefore, employed, when your performance continues to surpass your portion of the company's costs in you. This is called return on investment (ROI). As an employee, you are that investment. Understand, too, that the more you are paid, the more value you are proportionally required to deliver, which, of course, makes sense.

HOW YOU GENERATE REVENUE EVEN IF YOU DON'T

Most of the time, your accomplishments will not be earth-shattering. Most of the time, it's the stuff you do—and do well—as a normal, maybe even routine, part of your daily work that you should focus on when seeking to identify personal accomplishments. Consider that for a minute.

I don't want you to be one of those people who have trouble figuring out how they can quantify their value. Just look a little closer at what you do. If you are being kept on the job, you are generating value. Accept that.

When you think about your organization, how many people do you think are actively involved daily in generating revenue? The correct answer is all of them, you included. But, for the sake of illustration, let's say it's just the sales team.

Most companies are comprised of folks who support the sales and delivery of a product or service: front-end admin, manufacturing, service providers, inventory, shipping, billing, payroll, et cetera. That nothing happens in business until somebody sells something is a constant in the world of business. But once something is sold, it takes a lot of people working in concert to make the delivery. And generally, nobody gets paid until delivery is completed. What this means is, even though most people may not be salespeople, their services can still be quantified in dollars and percentages. To prove this, I often ask, "How would your employer know what to pay you if your value could not be quantified?"

9 Your Employer Is Not Responsible for Pointing Out Your Wins

YOU GO TO WORK. You work hard. You get paid. You go home. You get up the next day and do it all over again, but your company gets to keep your big wins under wraps? *Wha—?* Well, yes. If they choose to do so. (PS: This next sentence is yellow-highlighter worthy.) To determine your Quotient, your personal value for a specific period of time, *you are solely responsible for sourcing your achievements.*

Owners take the big risk of launching a business and, when successful, are entitled to a big reward. And because they did such a good job, you get to work there. This does not mean they are required to point out and share with you every valuable accomplishment you have if you don't recognize its value.

You would have to agree with me that for both parties, employee and employer, it's much better when an employee contributes value (far) in excess of his or her current rate of pay. This causes profit to happen. Most of my job-search and promotion-seeking clients—even those with outrageous QTNT PVCs—were unaware of having accomplished as much as they did until well after we mutually worked to discover what they had *actually* achieved on the job. A lot of eyes were opened. And whose fault was that? It was theirs! There is no going back to former employers to request a bonus or a commission on a five-year-old achievement. Looking back, I recognize wins in my own past for which I should have been more richly rewarded, but I missed them. My bad. And my loss.

SHOULD YOUR EMPLOYER INFORM YOU OF YOUR OUTSTANDING QUOTIENT SCORE?

This naturally leads to another question: Does an employer have the responsibility to inform an employee that he or she has achieved a personal value calculation higher than an =1? Or even a 1? The short answer is no. The longer answer resides in the following Rick Gillis proclamation:

> *It is the company's right to benefit, indeed prosper, from the outrageously creative and financially beneficial efforts of its employees, whether those employees recognize the value of their work or not.*

> *Further, the company has no responsibility to point out said gains realized by individuals employed by the company when those individuals are not engaged or diligent enough to recognize the extraordinary value of their own, specific contribution to the company.*

In plain old English, management is not *required* to recognize, bonus, or promote anyone. That does not mean it won't happen. Bonuses and promotions happen every day. But did you get yours? And, more to the point, was it in line with your contribution?

A paycheck and any commissions or bonuses previously agreed upon at the time of acceptance of an offer of employment are all an employer is required to pay an employee, regardless of whether a job was simply well done or whether it was over-the-top, *exceptionally* well done. This means it's up to you and nobody else to demonstrate how much your company benefits from your over-the-top, shout-at-the-top-of-your-lungs performance. The Quotient achieves this.

Mateo: VP, Bank Marketing
"You saved the bank."

Mateo had recently retired from a bank in Texas. After just a few months, he figured out he wasn't cut out for golf. He attended one of my workshops, hoping to learn some new tactics to put himself back on the market. During the workshop, Mateo was so taken with the idea of learning whether he had done anything particularly special during his career that he decided to text ten former coworkers, including the bank's president, his former boss. He asked each of them what difference he might have made during the time they had worked together. Almost immediately, Mateo got a response from the president of the bank, saying he had "saved the bank."

What?

During the next break, Mateo ran out to call his former supervisor to ask him what the heck he was referring to.

At the time of Mateo's "saving the bank" (in the early 1990s), the US was in a national banking crisis, and the Resolution Trust Corporation (RTC) was shutting down and selling off undercapitalized banks. Mateo's bank was informed that, with no way of acquiring additional funds to meet reserve requirements, it was potentially in danger of being taken over by the federal agency and sold off.

While this was happening, Mateo had pitched a new retail product that his boss had given him the approval to market. Mateo created the program, managed the implementation, and sold it to the public. It was an overwhelming success. Without his knowing it, Mateo had saved the bank.

So why hadn't he been aware of this at the time? His boss, hoping to avert the crisis, had never said a word about the bank's dire situation to anyone who did not have a need to know. He feared it would shatter morale and that staff would jump ship. Then, after the situation was avoided, he figured, *Why mention it at all?*

The moral of the story is this: if Mateo had not asked his previous employer what impact he had made, he would never have known about his colossal accomplishment.

A RECORD QUOTIENT SCORE

At that time, I had not yet come up with the concept of the QTNT PVC, so I recently reached out to Mateo (who is now formally and forever retired) to ask just two questions: What was the approximate value of the bank at the time of this event, and what was his annual salary?

You might want to sit down for this one! This is my all-time whopper! (Well, so far.)

According to Mateo, at the time the bank was valued at approximately $1.3 billion, and he was earning $50,000 a year base (not counting bonus). Here's his personal value calculation:

$$\frac{\$1,300,000,000}{\$50,000} = 26,000$$

**Mateo's QTNT PVC score for this
project was 26,000 (times his annual pay)!**

Yes, I know this number must be "sliced and diced" all kinds of ways, and of course all hands were on deck; Mateo did not pull this off by himself. *But he was the person who conceived of a retail banking product that was suc-cessful enough to generate the needed revenue to fend off the feds during a critical time in the bank's history.*

*"Accomplishments are the currency
of your career."*

—RICK GILLIS

10 Your Accomplishments Inventory

A S YOU NOW know, your employer—heck, your immediate supervisor—is not responsible for pointing out your wins; you are. How do you do this? With a simple process I created several years ago for my clients: the Accomplishments Inventory. From this written record of your personal best achievements, you will be able to create an Accomplishments Statement worthy of being presented to anyone in authority whenever and wherever the occasion may arise. There is a sample Accomplishments Inventory in appendix II for your review.

My reason for creating this process and the resulting document was twofold: First, my clients needed to be reminded that the work they had produced previously was valuable; and second, they needed to look deeper to see if those contributions could be quantified. It's just not enough to say you did something. The result must be presented in the language of your audience—usually in dollars made or saved.

Many times, these professionals knew what they had *done*, but it was not uncommon for them to learn of results far beyond what they believed they had *achieved*. The true value of some of these efforts would not come to light until we put pencil to paper. You have already seen some of those results in the Q-Studies.

HOW THE PROCESS WORKS

You may think sourcing your accomplishments is a no-brainer, right? Well, not necessarily. It depends on how much of your personal work history you have available to you, how good your memory is, and where you currently find yourself on your career journey.

For those of you able to get by on recent accomplishments, you probably don't need to search much further than your calendar or recent performance appraisals. More experienced and mature employees may feel they can get by with current wins—and this may be true if you have had some outrageously killer accomplishments lately. Even so, looking back over your personal history will provide you with greater leverage. Experience has value. How you wish to express that and how far back you decide to go is up to you.

In any case, here is a simple, three-step process that will help you start sourcing your best on-the-job wins:

1. Identify a problem you solved or an idea you had that improved a process or situation. Describe it in detail. Write down everything you can think of that addresses the who, what, where, when, why, and how of the situation. You can't have too much detail.
2. Describe the solution, also using as much detail as possible.
3. Calculate and describe the value you generated for your company.

One more thing: During this exploratory phase, everything is significant. If you think it might have value for your list, write it down. You can always toss it later.

OTHER PEOPLE'S MEMORIES

There are two ways to track down accomplishments: your memory and other people's memories. Begin with your own by reviewing performance reports. They are gold! If you are in the military or a veteran, you should have copies of every report ever generated about you.

Next, look at résumés or curriculum vitae (CV). Résumés are good for reminding you of the specific things you did and the responsibilities you held while on a previous job. Online calendars and organizers can be an incredible source of former contacts, projects, and events in which you were involved.

Next, begin asking family—yes, family! They will remind you of all kinds of wins you have told them about over the years. Be sure to ask your mom. Your mom remembers everything good you have ever told her. Follow up with current and former supervisors, clients, customers, vendors, friends, and associates.

INCLUDE DETAILS

As your list of accomplishments grows, start adding detail behind each bullet. Tell a story. During an interview or performance review, when you are asked how you accomplished something, be prepared to go into the specifics without ever breaking eye contact.

You must be credible in stating precisely what you achieved and how the company received a specific value from your efforts. Keep your audience in mind, and speak in a manner you know he or she will appreciate. Lead with the result. Impressing your immediate supervisor is your preliminary goal, but you should always be thinking of at least one manager above your boss with whom you will be sharing your achievement.

11 The Defensible Statement and the Perfect Elevator Pitch

SALES ARE EASY to measure. Everything else, not so much. This is where your working knowledge of what you accomplish on the job in concert with the Quotient can show that you know what you're talking about, even when you don't have access to hard facts and figures.

A few years back, I created what I call the Defensible Statement to address this issue. I have used this statement myself when attempting to describe a personal achievement when I don't have any hard numbers in hand. You probably have, too. Previously, I mentioned the use of acceptable workarounds for calculating the value of various achievements. These work hand in hand with the Defensible Statement.

For example, you might know the approximate average salary rate for your work team, and you claim to have saved your team of ten people ten hours of work per week. You guesstimate the average pay for your group to be $25 to $30 an hour. Rather than choose to use an average of the two rates, I would recommend you claim an even lower pay rate for your group—say, $20 an hour—to be comfortably conservative, and defensible, with your numbers. This reduces the chance that you will be confronted by management with an overstated value.

By using the $20-per-hour rate, you claim a $2,000 weekly savings times fifty or fifty-two weeks per year. You have just come up with a significant value that is justifiable, conservative, and defensible to your bosses. For an idea of how this might look in the "real world," see Q-Study No. 6 and Q-Study No. 12 in this book. Allen, a construction superintendent, had only a salary factor to work with but was, nevertheless, able to come up with some verifiably significant and defensible savings calculations.

Without exact figures, it is important to present your statement so that its validity will not be questioned. You must be able to comfortably defend it. Besides, your boss or your boss's boss may know the actual numbers, right?

THE PERFECT ELEVATOR (OR ANYWHERE ELSE) PITCH

You might wonder why I would decide that this is the right place in the book to bring up the on-the-job elevator pitch. The answer is this: now that you know how to craft a Defensible Statement, you need a great place to share it. But why the elevator when you can share this kind of stuff anywhere—and should? Because I'm interested in pointing out the parameter here: those twenty or thirty valuable seconds you have to prove to someone important how wonderful you are.

This pitch is entirely different from the job search pitch of the same name because here you can't use the same statement over and over and over and over. This little "speech" needs to be current and relevant. Yes, this is another small item to be tracking in the back of your mind, but we're talking about your professional job progression here.

The scenario: Wonderful you enters the elevator with your face buried in your phone. You reach out to choose your floor and happen to notice someone else is in the elevator with you. It's *just* your division SVP. What do you say? "Grand weather we're having"? Or worse—*nothing*? This is an opportunity to leverage yourself Quotient-style. How? By being prepared to talk about the topic you know best: you and your accomplishments.

Notice I said "prepared," as in prepared to share a delightful statement about how something you did recently saved the company a gob of money. If you have calculated an approximate QTNT PVC in support of your statement and can share the specific (or defensible) value of your effort for the good of the company, begin the celebration! Fact: Senior management loves to hear about their employees' wins. Your wins are their wins too.

For example, after the requisite greetings are complete, you can anticipate your SVP may say something like "What have you been up to?" This is the opening you are seeking. And it's your turn to say, "I'm really pleased to tell you I was able to shave a few hours a week off a couple of routine processes in the accounting office. It looks like the result will be savings to the company in the neighborhood of five to six hundred dollars per week, every week, for the rest of the year."

Do you think this might initiate a "How did you do that?" kind of response?

Q-STUDY NO. 5

Mariana: Paralegal/Administrative Assistant

"Breathing Life into Stagnant Files"

Mariana was a paralegal working for a century-old US law firm with offices in several countries. Over the decades, as cases were finalized, relevant files and exhibits were dispatched to a storeroom in the home office where, as the need arose, they were sought out for review. This was an ongoing need that occurred more often than one might think.

At the time of her accomplishment, Mariana had been with the firm for several years. The firm, knowing the high quality of her work, assigned her the job of copying, digitizing, converting, and/or photographing all of the content that had become the "dead file" storage center. The space required to house all this stuff had, over time, expanded to take up two floors of the firm's corporate office tower. Lawyers, clerks, and secretaries wasted valuable time and resources seeking out files and/or exhibits when needed for review.

Mariana was provided with a budget to hire a team of six temp workers and acquire the equipment needed to complete the project. Within one year, Mariana was able to hand over the keys to the physical master files and successfully provide the firm with access to the same files in digital form.

MARIANA'S QTNT SCORE

During her research for this achievement, Mariana spoke with the firm's CFO, who provided her with a then-current average staff-hour rate of $400 per hour. The CFO also told her that the company had seen approximately three hundred staff hours saved weekly due to the efficiencies of her system. At the time of this accomplishment, Mariana's annual salary was $48,000. We now have enough information to determine Mariana's PVC for this one event.

The numbers we have to work with:

$400 per staff-hour saved due to the benefits of online access to what had previously been physical files

300 staff-hours weekly "returned" to the firm

$400 savings x 300 staff-hours = $120,000 in weekly savings
$120,000 x 52 weeks per year = $6,240,000 per year in savings

$$\frac{\text{Total savings} = \$6,240,000}{\text{Mariana's salary} = \$48,000} = 130$$

Mariana's QTNT rating for this year of performance = 130

From the firm's point of view, all costs would be taken into account to come up with their own cost/savings benefit. But with the CFO having provided Mariana with an hourly benefit to the company, Mariana can be proud of her achievement and defend her QTNT score as stated.

There are other wins associated with Mariana's work. Her manager(s) would have also recognized that she

- had the leadership skills necessary to manage a team of six temps, because there is no question she would have had to deal with the transitory nature of her staff and deal with the turnover and the necessary training involved to get each replacement up to speed;

- was attentive to detail;

- was knowledgeable of the lingo and legal cataloging;

- was knowledgeable of the digital processes and the associated software;

- made previously difficult-to-access archival data reliably retrievable;

- created savings and the potential to generate new revenue due to the recovery of 15,600 work hours (300 hours/week x 52 weeks); and

- delivered outstanding value in return for her pay.

Here is how Mariana recounted this accomplishment when given the opportunity to speak about it:

This project took one year and a team of six temporary, full-time employees to complete. Besides managing the team, I was responsible for the digital transference of all paper and microfiche files, including the photography, identification, and storage of all physical evidence accumulated by the law firm over the decades.

Based on an average rate of $400 (provided by CFO) per staff-hour, I saved the firm $120,000 per week (based on the reduction of an average of three hundred staff-hours of weekly access to the historical files by staff x $400), or $6,240,000 annually ($120,000 x 52 weeks). This project came in on time and budget.

Undoubtedly, she would be closely questioned over details such as the allotted budget and how much was spent on temps, equipment, software, IT support, implementation, et cetera. She would be asked about the difficulties or snags she encountered and how she resolved those problems, turning the "bad and the ugly" into gold.

12 The Quotient and Soft Skills

A FRIEND OF MINE, someone not in management, was at work when a lunchtime shooting occurred in her multistory office building. Management was out of the office, and guests waiting on their return were in a small conference room off the lobby.

My friend received a call from a peer on another floor that there was an active shooter in the building. She immediately escorted the waiting guests into the secure office area and began walking the floor, gathering employees. The entire group hunkered down to wait for the all-clear.

This story is an example of the finest and most important of soft skills being put to use: leadership and the ability to take charge. In this case, I could also add "keeping calm under extreme pressure." The person in this story had no managerial authority, but it didn't matter. She took command of the situation and did what needed to be done at the moment. Fortunately, no one in her suite of offices was hurt.

The Quotient does not make an allowance for soft skills in the calculation of an individual's score. Nevertheless, and I don't think I should have to say this, every individual and every manager must take soft skills into consideration when rating or ranking any employee or preparing their own Quotient calculation. Perhaps we should call this the defensible-skills aspect of the QTNT PVC.

THE VALUE OF SOFT SKILLS

Soft skills are broadly defined as those skills that complement hard skills. These can include social, communication, and people skills as well as attitude and emotional intelligence. Others include etiquette, flexibility, personal motivation, accountability, self-discipline, professional appearance, creativity, and the willingness to take initiative and work hard. Someone who plays well with others has strong soft skills. Looking at these qualities, it's easy to see why people with great soft skills make great employees.

When talking about personal performance on the job, there is never a wrong time to bring up an employee's soft skills—or to examine your own. These skills add intrinsic value to job performance. Do not discount your soft skills when it comes to calculating your Quotient. If they do not fit anywhere into the calculation, don't be afraid to highlight these skills in your narrative on paper or in person.

In the event you and a coworker are being considered for promotion and the two of you are, for the most part, equal in the eyes of management—and further, your Quotient scores are very similar—a soft-skills inventory could be the tiebreaker. Be prepared to speak to those intrinsic skills you possess that lie outside the job description.

13 Quantification of Achievement

AS YOU REVIEW Q-Studies, you can see how I calculated each QTNT score step-by-step. In every case, I asked my clients to think about what they had accomplished on the job in terms of the *value received* by the company or client after all costs and expenses were deducted. I bring this to your attention because this is the very first step in measuring your own value. I appreciate that, as an employee, you may not have access to those costs to determine your value contribution, in which case, you need to get creative and identify your own best management-acceptable workarounds. However, before doing that, let's go online.

ONLINE SEARCH

The internet is porous. Somewhere, somehow, by design or by mistake, the information you want can generally be found online. Cost and expense information, even if just generic to your industry, is not confidential.

Talking with several active and former chief financial officers, I was surprised to discover how many big organizations make operating cost information available internally to those employees who need it to do their jobs—and, somewhat by extension, to those who actively seek it out. This means that the data you need to calculate your Quotient might be available to you right at your workstation.

It is important to note that any information on company systems is, first of all, confidential—no matter how easy it may be to access. Secondly, a company system only reflects transactional information. If what you want to learn is not captured statistically by the company accounting system, then it won't be found online in-house. This is one reason why we will continue to talk about workarounds. When you are reviewing Q-Studies, try to "read between the lines" to see how my conclusions may inspire your thinking.

On the other side of this coin, there was one particular CFO who, having been with divisions of three Fortune 100 companies, stated emphatically that there was no way her former companies would have shared this kind of internal information with anyone who did not have a documented need to know. If this is the case where you work, that will oblige us to seek out those workarounds with enough of the *right* kind of information necessary for you to establish a *defensible value* for what you currently do for your company.

SMALL BUSINESSES MAY NOT SHARE INFORMATION

One small business owner I spoke with told me there was no chance he was going to share his financials with anyone but his accountant, his banker, and the IRS—and I accept that.

Although this owner was ultimately successful, there were months, especially in the early days, when he took home nothing for himself after making payroll for what eventually came to be thirty full-time employees. Like most small business owners, he did not share good *or* bad information with his workers. Over time, as he was able to generate a solid return on his hard work, risk, and investment, he was finally able to pay himself well. This is, after all, what being an entrepreneur is all about.

From my point of view and the small business point of view, this argument makes all the sense in the world. The smaller the business, the less likely an owner will share confidential information with employees. Nevertheless, as you will see later in the book, this does not mean that the Quotient can't still be utilized by small business.

Allen: Construction/
The Cement Pour

"They wouldn't give me the numbers!"

Allen is a highly successful, world-class construction superintendent. At the time we began working together, he was unable to provide me with the operating costs necessary to determine his contribution on a job site because the company would not make those costs available "to the field." (What?)

On one particular job, he was in charge of two separate but identical concrete foundation pours that would become the bases for two freestanding superstructures. He told me that, due to his extensive note-taking, as well as photographing virtually every stage of the initial pour as it took place, he had been able to generate a 30% savings on the second pour. However—and this is important—he was unable to establish a dollar value for these savings that he could present to anyone in, or out of, the company.

After listening to the details of the project, I was able to point out to Allen that he did indeed have enough information at his disposal to find a partial but reasonable Quotient for this segment of the overall project. Notice that I said "partial."

The PVC that follows, based on the information at hand, would have been more accurate had he been able to access all costs associated with the job (i.e., transportation, materials, facilities, inventory, training, etc.). But, as you will see, in terms of his Quotient score, this works to Allen's benefit. However, he must be prepared to explain to anyone that this score was outrageously high because the necessary accounting information was unavailable to him.

THE WORKAROUND

Both foundations were required to be flawless—perfectly level and without any cracks or voids. Allen and his team executed perfectly on both pours. Since he couldn't find a way to measure the savings between the two, I asked him three questions based on information I knew he would have:

1. How many workers were on-site for each pour? *He said between one thousand and twelve hundred. I chose to use one thousand.*
2. Taking the average of the highest and the lowest hourly rate, what was the average pay for those thousand workers? *$40 per hour.*
3. How long did the *first* pour take? *Forty hours nonstop.*

I told Allen we now had all the information we would need. Remember that the calculations that follow are based solely on his workers' average hourly rate of pay. No other costs are included. Although what follows is certainly not a cost accountant's entry, it is a methodology you can learn from that will help you understand how you, too, can creatively quantify a reasonable dollar value for your work.

First, we will determine the on-site salary expense not including any overtime:

1,000 workers x $40 x 40 hours = $1,600,000
This number represents the approximate gross
salary expense for the first pour.

All we have to do now is multiply the total salary expense for this first pour by 30%—the amount Allen told me he had saved on the identical second pour.

$1,600,000 x .30 = $480,000 = value of Allen's contribution

Therefore, $480,000 represents the number of salary dollars only that Allen saved on this job over the course of the two identical foundation pours.

You might be wondering, as I did, how Allen came up with a 30% time-saved factor over the first pour. The simple answer is that he and his team accomplished the second pour in twenty-eight hours, or 30% (40 x .30 = 12) fewer hours than it took to execute the initial pour.

DETERMINING ALLEN'S QTNT SCORE

At the time this work was accomplished, Allen's (base) pay was $95,000 per year. Were we to divide $480,000 by $95,000, we would arrive at a QTNT PVC of 5.05, but this would not be accurate because Allen's pay rate in this calculation is an *annual* figure, and the work being described here was accomplished in *hours*.

To arrive at an accurate Quotient for this project, we need to take Allen's $95,000 annual pay and convert it to an hourly rate. To do this, we will divide his annual pay by 2,080—the number of work hours in a year based on a forty-hour workweek.

$95,000 ÷ 2080 = $45.67 = Allen's hourly rate

Knowing Allen's hourly rate, we can now calculate his pay for the forty-hour first pour.

40 hours x $45.67 = $1,826.80

Taking into account that the second pour only took twenty-eight hours, we need to add those salary dollars to the amount above.

28 hours (40 hours reduced by 30%) x $45.67 = $1,278.76
This is Allen's pay for the 28-hour second pour.

$1,826.80 + $1,278.76 = $3,105.56
Allen earned a total of $3,105.56 for his combined 68 hours of work.

With this information, we can now calculate Allen's QTNT PVC for both pours.

Total value delivered (based on salary savings only)   = $480,000
Total pay Allen earned for these two jobs   = $3,105.56

Allen's QTNT PVC score for this project = 154.56

Very impressive! You can look forward to seeing another one of Allen's accomplishments on this same job later in the book. That one deals in minutes saved.

14 The Net Result

BESIDES SAYING YOU deserve more money for all the time you put in, can you identify the financial benefit your company receives as a result of all that time you put in?

You may not work on commission or be in sales, but you deliver benefit to your company, or you wouldn't be there. Throughout the book you might have noticed that I have been nudging you to think about the value of your contributions to your company much like a salesperson would, and how to calculate a net result for each claim you make and share that result with your supervisors.

Rare is the non-sales worker who can provide the *financially* beneficial results of their work, which, truthfully, makes a lot of sense since we usually let "accounting" take care of that. But therein lies the problem. *You* have to be able to tell your employer how you make or save the company money.

THE CURRENCY OF YOUR CAREER

Good job performance may not be enough to get you noticed by those who matter most. Maybe your work does not speak for itself, so let's make certain that *you* do. How? By getting into the habit of informing your bosses (all of them) about your on-the-job wins. That was not a typo. I meant to say "bosses"—plural—because you need to be comfortable speaking to your boss about your achievements as well as—politics aside—her boss and his boss. You need to be able to speak to anyone, anywhere up the chain of command, about how you contribute value. Immediate supervisors come and go. You want to be the first one considered for the position when yours takes off or is promoted.

I have mentioned this earlier, but I don't think you can hear it too often: To achieve the confidence to speak to all bosses anytime and anywhere, you must embrace my "What and Wow!" rule of the employment jungle:

Every accomplishment must end with a net result.

This is a hard-and-fast rule when stating accomplishments. Telling someone about the actions you took without sharing the result is like telling a joke without a punchline. Remember, too, that when your boss is listening, somewhere inside her brain, she is calculating what it cost the company for you to achieve what you did.

I WAS RESPONSIBLE FOR _____ THAT RESULTED IN _____.

Read that line out loud—"*I was responsible for BLANK that resulted in BLANK*"—and it will make more sense to you. Now try it again the way I originally presented this statement to you– "*I was responsible for WHAT that resulted in WOW.*"

Do you see how much more significant this is than just saying, "I did (blank)"? To an employer or a manager, that just doesn't mean anything. You might as well tell them you filled the copy machine with paper.

While I will always encourage you to provide the Wow in dollars, the result does not have to be stated in revenue—especially if you don't have any idea what that amount might be. You can use percentages, such as "decreased time to market by 3%," or you can just use good old plain descriptive adjectives, such as "decreased time to market *significantly*." The point here is that you must be able to state *why* what you did is important to your employer. Take a look at this statement:

"I was responsible for <u>creating a new screening procedure</u> that resulted in <u>60 fewer hours spent monthly on warranty claims</u>."

Exactly how you say it is not as important as the Wow in your statement.

15 Formatting Accomplishments for Presentation

YOUR ACCOMPLISHMENTS STATEMENT, in final presentation, is meant to be as formal and professionally attractive as a résumé or CV. Get your supervisor's attention with the appearance and then knock their socks off with the content.

ORGANIZING YOUR ACCOMPLISHMENTS STATEMENT

Depending on where and to whom you are presenting this document, you may want to include your job title, location within the organization, telephone number, and email address. Always make it easy for someone up the ladder to be able to contact you.

Below the header, without any explanation (none is necessary), begin to list the accomplishments you consider the most valuable for your supervisor(s) to recognize. It doesn't matter if the person you report to already knows this information. Sometimes re-ringing a bell can have an impact.

List your accomplishments using the Accomplishments Inventory formula: Accomplishment + "resulting in" + Value Statement.

Organize your accomplishments in the order you feel will make the biggest impact on your audience. This is something you will do based on your job, what your boss expects of you, and the inside knowledge you have from being in the environment.

Notice in the sample Accomplishments Statement (appendix I) that accomplishments are not numbered. This is by design so that no one accomplishment appears more important than any other. Besides, you are going to put your most notable and current accomplishment in the first position, followed by the next most important in the second, and so forth. By using bullets instead of numbers, you do not grant one accomplishment more value than another. On the other hand, this is your document. If you prefer to number them, go for it!

Double-space between each accomplishment to make this page "breathe." You don't want clutter. White space allows each accomplishment to be scanned quickly by your audience. It also enables it to stand on its own merits and invites discussion.

HOW MANY?

In theory there is no limit—no right number of accomplishments to include in this document. In reality, however, there is probably a protocol dictated by your company's culture. You will "know" what the right number is. If you are in sales, two or more pages may be appropriate. Any other occupation will most likely be best served by presenting a single page. Stick with your intuition on this one. You never want to come off as boastful, but you do want appropriate attention. The tastefully correct number will win the day.

Your goal is to see that decision-makers are aware of the value you bring to the organization. All your work in gathering and writing your accomplishments, organizing them into a compelling list, maintaining that list, and creating a clean, clear presentation will get the job done.

Lynne: Account Manager
"Saving the Account"

I met Lynne in a workshop I presented. A few days later, she sent me an email sharing an accomplishment she was proud of for my consideration. I very much like this accomplishment because it reinforces the idea that just doing what you do and doing it well can be an accomplishment in its own right.

Lynne was a rock star with a global player in the electronic print services industry. Her statement below succinctly sums up her achievement in my "What and Wow!" format, after which she goes on to describe the "save" in the same sort of detail she would use when discussing this issue with senior management.

Here's what she did and how she did it:

Rescued a troubled program implementation for [a Fortune 500 client], resulting in $50,000,000 in revenue and the retention of the client.

Here is her unedited story:

Most of the accomplishment was convincing client management that I cared about the business relationship.

The Situation: The external client was getting ready to cancel their agreement for a Managed Print Services solution implementation and a five-year on-going support contract. The contract was valued at $10,000,000 annually. This was a strategic client with a long relationship with the company, and we were on the verge of being kicked out of the account. The client was mad that the project was behind schedule, and they questioned our ability to deliver the value of the business solution they had purchased. I was managing a project management office at the time, and because the project was high profile and the relationship with the client was so strained, I assigned the project to myself.

What Did I Do? I got the project back on track.

How Did I Do It? I immediately forged a trusting relationship with the senior vice president (who was the business sponsor). I handled yet another mistake that was made by the company (this one was caught on camera) two days after I arrived on-site in Manhattan.

Re-scoped the client requirements; rewrote the implementation contract; re-baselined the project scope, schedule, and cost; documented the roles and responsibilities and necessary skill sets of the personnel working on the project implementation and the personnel who would provide on-going support; recommended the addition of a very senior-level network architect to the project team; and recommended the replacement of several support personnel.

Gained agreement from the executive management of the company I worked for and the client to move forward with the new project plan. When the project was back on track, I turned it over to one of the project managers on my staff, and the implementation and on-going support were ultimately very successful.

Benefit of My Actions? *Saved my company $50,000,000 in revenue and kept the client relationship.*

LYNNE'S QUOTIENT(S)

Based on the information we have, we know Lynne saved the contract in the first year of the five-year agreement. At the time, her salary was $125,000 per year. Here is that calculation:

$$\frac{\text{Single-year value of the account Lynne saved} = \$10,000,000}{\text{Lynne's annual salary} = \$125,000}$$

Lynne's QTNT score for saving this account = 80

If, however, Lynne were to decide to present this accomplishment as having saved the *entire* $50,000,000 account in this single year, she *might* (note italics) be able to present her PVC calculation to her managers like this:

$$\frac{\text{Total value of the account over 5 years} = \$50,000,000}{\text{Lynne's salary} = \$125,000}$$

Lynne's QTNT score for saving the (entire) account = 400

Admittedly, this is a stretch, but her bosses might agree she did save the entire five-year agreement from the dustbin, "allowing" her to make this claim.

16

Speaking About You

WANT YOU TO be comfortable with *casually on purpose* dropping short, rehearsed (yes, rehearsed!) statements on your boss (and your boss's boss and her boss as well) to let them in on your little secret: you deliver like they never knew!

We all know of someone who was terminated because the company was unaware of the quality or quantity of their contributions. Whose fault is that? The worker? Yes. Their manager and immediate supervisors? Also yes.

If you are already comfortable talking about what you do and how well you do it, then good for you. But if you are the reserved type who will not even toot your own horn to family, well then, prepare thyself for some game-changing mental adjustments.

HOW TO SPEAK THE LANGUAGE OF "YOU"

You can begin your practice of personal on-the-job promotion by *consciously* dropping small wins on a close friend or coworker. Consider this practice. Pay attention to what and how you talk about your job with friends after work at the watering hole. Notice how comfortable you are telling them you _____ (insert accomplishment here). You aren't boasting (well, maybe you are, a little!). But mostly you are communicating, sharing.

Now take that same accomplishment and "convert" it to manager-speak—the language you would use on the job to describe the same achievement. Remember, you are informing—for your benefit.

Pay attention to your mindset. Note how comfortable you are with your friends. Pay attention to your body language and your facial expression. Notice how easy this is to do because *you are the expert*. You know your stuff. This is the lesson to be learned. Continue to practice with other coworkers, friends, and family.

Next, take this effort up a notch and repeat these same small wins with your immediate supervisor. Strive to get to the point, the value statement—the punchline—quickly. Brief is good. If what you have to say is interesting, your audience will ask for more information. That's when you will know you are on the right track! After a few practice rounds, you will find yourself getting more and more comfortable speaking about you. This is not only good training; it will also reinforce your accomplishments mindset.

Now that you have tested some of your statements, you can use the same strategy when you run into that senior vice president in the hallway. Notice how well your message is received. Don't be concerned because you think what you do is not important enough for a VP. They will appreciate your candor.

As you become more skilled at sharing your wins with those around you, think of it as performance review practice. The time to speak up on your own behalf is when you sit down with your boss for a professional review of your performance. That is the place where those discussions about pay and promotion begin.

17

Accomplishments as a Tool: Where to Share

NTERESTINGLY, IT IS a very real possibility that, in the course of your career, you may never actually present a formal written Accomplishments Statement to a supervisor. This assumes you are consistently able to seize the opportunity for a one-on-one discussion. However, this possibility *does not* permit you to avoid preparing a formal document for other eventualities—in particular, performance reviews. (Candidly, the Accomplishments Statement is my "secret sauce" tactic when advising job and advancement seekers on how to land their next position up to and including the C-suite.)

As you review the various ways to share your wins below, remember that at any time you can expect to have to explain the QTNT PVC. You may have to speak in terms of the *multiples* (x times your pay) of value your employer received for your work, which is, of course, what the Quotient represents.

Next, we should think about the places where you can share this information for your benefit.

PERFORMANCE APPRAISAL AND SEEKING PROMOTION

Having the knowledge and ability to present and defend calculations confirming that you exceeded the value produced by your competition (your coworkers) can be the compelling difference at bonus time and in getting the promotion.

SEEKING A RAISE

Similar to seeking promotion, your QTNT PVC score could be all the justification you need to make the case that you are entitled to a performance-based pay raise.

OBTAINING A BONUS

Occasionally, you may have a singularly outstanding year (or quarter, or month, etc.). It is not unreasonable to assume you may see an opportunity to speak up for yourself and obtain a bonus. Knowing your score can go a long way to help you "stand your ground" for a bonus in line with your achievement.

For example, while calculating your PVC, you figure you saved the company $50,000 this year doing whatever it is you do. If a salesperson generated this kind of revenue, he or she may be entitled to a 10% commission, or $5,000, for their efforts. But let's say you are an inventory manager—a position not normally bonused. Knowing your Quotient rate for this unusual achievement and pointing it out could generate some unanticipated cash.

NEGOTIATING A SALARY OFFER

I encourage you to go back and do your best to determine your Quotient for your most recent positions. Knowing these scores for previous jobs puts you in a position to sell yourself and negotiate from an *informed* point of view.

PROPER PAY FOR PERFORMANCE/PAY EQUALITY

I will be talking about pay for performance in chapter 19, "Equal Pay or the Proper Pay?"

AGE DISCRIMINATION AND MID-TO-LATE CAREER PROFESSIONALS

In my experience, fifty-year-old or older workers are especially vulnerable to getting the ax when they least expect it. Age discrimination begins for women at about the age of thirty-five (yes, this is true; sorry) and for men at around age forty. The next generation is right behind you and gunning for your position. Until you retire, you can never quit speaking value to your performance. The Quotient supports your doing so.

DEFENDING YOUR POSITION DURING A LAYOFF

Knowing your QTNT PVC is powerful and can be especially useful during layoffs. You must have the ability to stand up before the powers that be and inform them, with supporting data, that terminating you means X amount of dollars will go out the door. This could be an eye-opener for those who are about to let you go. Minds can be changed.

JOB SEARCH

Knowing your Quotient for all of your past positions, or at least your most recent one, will go a long way toward getting that job offer over the competition. This is where the multiples-of-base-pay discussion comes in handy.

18 Your Accomplishments and Your QTNT Score

REFERRING TO THE sample Accomplishments Inventory for Janet Best, in appendix II, you will notice the first two achievements have Quotient scores and the next one has a Q = 1. Others have no score. For these, Janet may not have been able to access the necessary information to calculate the score.

The obvious reason that certain accomplishments have a Quotient score is because a specific amount of revenue was realized by the organization and attributed to Janet's efforts. Of course, you do not see her rate of pay in her bulleted statements, but it's easy enough to reverse the math and determine that her pay at the time was $150,000 ($6,000,000 ÷ Q40 = $150,000).

Janet's most recent accomplishments—those she would be sharing with her current employer—would be those she has realized in her current position. In the event her Accomplishments Inventory is presented at a performance review, the accomplishments would only consist of current performance. This does not mean she can't include various accomplishments from previous positions she has held, but there would have to be an "informational" reason to include them (e.g., to indicate this is not the first time she has accomplished said goal).

The way I see it, one day, just a few short years into the future, after the Quotient concept becomes accepted as a means of rating and ranking, every position on a résumé, on an Accomplishments Statement, and even in professional social media profiles will have QTNT Personal Value Contribution scores attached to them.

Will some people want to "game the system" with artificial Quotient ratings? Sure. However, when those people are required to share the what, where, when, why, and how behind each score, their deceit will become apparent

"TRIGGERS AND COOL STORIES"
AN ACCOMPLISHMENTS INVENTORY QUICK START

I found myself speaking one day with California-based career advisor Mike McRitchie, who explained to me how he uses my accomplishments inventory process with his clients. I liked his take on the process so much that I asked if he would allow me to share it with you. Mike's very user-friendly version of sourcing accomplishments appears in appendix I.

Q-STUDY NO. 8

Anthony: Captain, US Navy

"Meritorious Unit Commendation"

I had the good fortune to advise a retiring US Navy Captain (O-6) before his departure from a thirty-year military career just prior to the launch of his civilian career. Anthony approached me about landing his ideal civilian job. Employing my "secret sauce" job search advice, I had him create a draft of his very best, personal, on-the-job accomplishments, exactly as I have coached you to do in this book.

As any active-duty or US military veteran can tell you, military personnel have copies of annual performance reports that list previous accomplishments, which makes this auditing exercise so much easier to implement. (I still have mine from my time in the US Air Force.) Anthony's description of his final duties allowed me to take the highlights and present them to you as if he were responding to a civilian interviewer's questions.

Since a lot of military accomplishments may or may not include dollar valuations, I asked the Captain if he could remember any specific achievements he could discuss in terms of dollars. As base commander responsible for final approval of all expenditures, this was not a stretch.

Below is his description of the last position he held before retiring as he originally presented it to me.

COMMANDING OFFICER, NAVAL AIR STATION DE (NOT ITS ACTUAL NAME)

Led efforts of 290 military/civilian employees in all aspects of operations and maintenance of a major naval air station with a $1,000,000,000 plant replacement value and an annual budget of $32,000,000. Responsible for all facilities, public works, utilities, airfield, and support activities of the installation. Planned and executed congressionally mandated base closure. Recognized by the Secretary of the Navy with the Meritorious Unit Commendation.

This statement led to the following "responsible for WHAT that resulted in WOW" Accomplishments Statement format:

Developed an aggressive schedule for the closure of Naval Air Station DE resulting in savings to the government of $3,620,000.

As you know, once you claim an accomplishment, it is your responsibility to provide the supporting background in defense of your achievement. I present this accomplishment to you in the format of a hiring manager questioning the Captain in a civilian interview.

Interviewer: How did you do that?
Due to our aggressive schedule for closure and disposal, caretaker costs over the two years since base closure were significantly under original estimates.

I: How did you arrive at $3,620,000?
The original estimate for caretaker costs for fiscal years (FY) 20XX and 20XX was $5,120,000. However, what was actually spent (including salaries, contract costs, utilities, and repairs) was under $1,500,000, resulting in savings to the government of $3,620,000.

I: What else can you tell me about this accomplishment?
Because these funds were budgeted into the future, these savings will continue to accumulate to the USN through FY XX. We were able to accomplish these savings because we put together an omnibus contract, laid away buildings instead of heating them during the winter, and disposed of 80% of the property well ahead of the forecast schedule, which got us out of the snow-plowing and mowing business.

At the time of this accomplishment, Anthony was making $135,000 annually, which we multiply by two as this was a two-year project.

$$\frac{\text{Savings realized by US Government } = \$3,620,000}{\text{The USN captain's annual salary x 2 } = \$270,000}$$

Anthony's QTNT score for this occurrence, which took place over two fiscal years = 13.4

Note that this single Quotient does not take into account any of the regular duties Anthony continued to perform as base commander. Based on his military history and management experience, Anthony had no problem landing a civilian job before departing the US Navy.

19

Equal Pay or
the Proper Pay?

ET'S SAY YOU and I work together. We do the same job, but I'm a
guy and you are a woman. Or I'm white and you're not. Or I'm young
and you aren't. I earn a Quotient of 7 for my work this year, and you
score a verifiable 23. We do not, at this time, know our respective scores.

A month passes, and you learn that I was promoted—on merit, *of
course*. But then, as such news tends to leak out in any work environment, you hear that my QTNT score for the previous year was a 7. Would
you have some kind of recourse after learning this?

I'm not an attorney, and I have not passed this by one for an opinion, but I feel fairly confident stating that—assuming all other qualifications are relatively similar if not equal—the Quotient illuminates the
pay disparity issue in such a way that you might want to have a talk with
someone in human resources—or the Equal Employment Opportunity
Commission (EEOC).

EQUAL PAY OR THE RIGHT PAY?

We hear a lot about equal pay and pay disparity—phrases that have their
place and that I will continue to use throughout the book—but I have a
different take on the bigger issue: Why are we talking about equal pay
when the Quotient is able to measure a return on investment (ROI)
in a way that has never been achievable in the past? Before the QTNT
Personal Value Calculation, we have never been able to mathematical-
ly measure the value of a contribution from any employee—woman or
man, disenfranchised or not. The Quotient changes all that.

How about, in addition to talking about equal pay, we talk about the
appropriate pay for performance? How about we talk about *proper pay*

for the value delivered? What if a woman's work product is more valuable than a man's in the same position? Does equal pay make her salary acceptable? I prefer that we—as both individuals and businesses, men and women, protected classes or not—seek fair pay for measurable value delivered. Isn't this how it works in sales? Yes. But don't get me wrong: I'm not suggesting non-sales professionals should be paid on a commission-type basis. On the contrary, my goal is to see that everyone learns how they add value to the organization, identify the extra value they deliver, defend it, and be paid accordingly. Will this take some education? You bet! That's why I have written this book and why you are reading and learning from it.

How about we modify the discussion somewhat and talk about the *proper pay for the value received* by the organization? Or, as I personally prefer to define it, the *proper pay for the best performance*. When you look at it that way, the Quotient is the defining (and very simple to calculate) determinant.

As I said above, I'm not suggesting a "commissioned" workforce. The market will determine the lowest rate anyone will be paid for their skills. Nevertheless, I advocate for anyone to have the opportunity to make more than the market floor suggests based on their *measurable* performance.

To be sure, this idea puts the onus on the employee to point out where she or he adds increased value. I have no problem saying out loud that it is the *motivated* employee who will benefit from working the QTNT PVC process.

CURRENTLY

In spite of legislation that requires equal pay for equal work, women, as I write this, earn approximately 80 cents on average for every dollar a man makes. That rate diminishes even further as a person's race or age is considered.

The Quotient is more than *just* an equalizer in the pay discussion. The QTNT PVC becomes the gold standard. It is up to the employer to reward those workers accordingly.

Of course there is more to the discussion of pay equity than just gender. Gender equality is only one of the several groups protected by law from employment discrimination. In fact, per the EEOC, *every* US citizen is a member of some protected class.

Discrimination of all kinds abounds in the workplace, and, unfortunately, due to human nature it always will. The Quotient may or may not change the way people think, but it will level the playing—or should I say "paying"?—field, no matter what our differences may be.

More pay, appropriate promotion, and bonuses for better work are the goals all individuals strive for. Conversely and appropriately, more production and bigger returns are the corporation's goals. This is a win-win, as we are all in this together.

Your engagement in the QTNT PVC process—that is, knowing what part you play in the bigger corporate picture and how you can personally quantify your contribution, no matter your role—should, I think, personally spur you on to produce more and provide a better quality of work. This process should also prove to you, as well as to management, that you already do more and better work than you are being recognized for.

REGARDING INDIVIDUAL RATE OF PAY

There are many reasonable variables that impact the rate of pay between two workers in the same space (e.g., experience, certifications, education, etc.). Knowing what you make and learning what everyone else around you makes may or may not make any difference. Where it does make a difference is when you learn that your equal-to or superior qualifications, advanced study, and experience are not reflected in your pay when compared to those who do the same work. This is where your engagement with the Quotient is inestimable.

Opening this chapter, I compared myself (a guy) and my score to a woman with a PVC far superior to mine, but I got the promotion. Perhaps that was based on the premise that I will make the better manager. Perhaps not. Maybe it had to do with the fact that I play golf and my coworker doesn't. Perhaps not . . .

ABOUT THAT 80¢

Think about this: Assuming men and women are doing the same work, if you divide a lower rate of pay into a comparable contribution value, the resulting Quotient will always be higher.

20 Parents, Teach Your Daughters to Negotiate

S EVERAL YEARS BACK, I worked with an attorney who was seeking a new opportunity. She had identified a startup she very much wanted to work for. Nettie had the talent and the work experience to support her candidacy; she was, in fact, perfect for the job. I prepped her for the interview and salary negotiations, keeping in mind that the company, at that particular moment in time, happened to consist of four men.

Nettie nailed the interview, and the guys called her back to discuss salary. She had a range in mind, and the offer came in at the exact bottom of her range. When we had discussed her strategy in advance, we assumed the offer would at least be in range, but I told her to beg off making a final decision on the spot. (I have always advised people to take a minimum of twenty-four hours before making a final decision on any offer, especially when it comes to pay. A Friday offer and a full weekend to think it over is the best!) Nettie was granted the delay and called me to discuss.

I congratulated her and told her to go back and negotiate for an increase. She was concerned. She told me the guys had met her minimum and that she didn't want to have the offer rescinded because of salary. I suggested—or rather, insisted—that she go back and negotiate. To address her concern that the deal might collapse, I prepped her with a fallback position: *If, during the negotiation, it began to look like the offer might be rescinded, she should stand up, say something about wanting to be part of the startup, put out her hand, and let them know she would accept their original offer.* This strategy made all the difference. Why? She had a fallback position and could focus instead on the negotiating aspect.

The next day I got a call from Nettie, who was over-the-top excited. She had negotiated and accepted a $15,000 increase to the original offer!

On another occasion, also with an attorney, I insisted she similarly counter the original offer based on my fallback strategy. She, too, was successful. The next day she got a call from the general counsel with whom she had negotiated. He told her he would have been disappointed if she had not countered his original offer.

I rest my case.

THE IMPORTANCE OF NEGOTIATING

People, you have to teach your daughters to negotiate. Over my years of working with women in job search and advancement, I have seen three truisms emerge:

1. Women (generally) don't negotiate a starting salary.
2. Women seldom ask for a raise.
3. Women rarely outright seek promotion.

For those women who do negotiate salary, do ask for raises and actively seek out promotions, please accept my apology. Nevertheless, I stand by my statement (thus, my use of the word *truism*—a generalization that, from experience, I know to be accurate).

The graph below offers a way to visualize why, when launching your career (for both men and women), negotiating your initial rate of pay is the only way to begin. Over time, as you can see, that first rate makes a big difference. Refer to the graph below while I discuss pay trajectory for a man and a woman doing the same job. We will assume all factors (education, age, internships, etc.) to be similar at the outset.

GENDER LIFETIME PAY COMPARISON

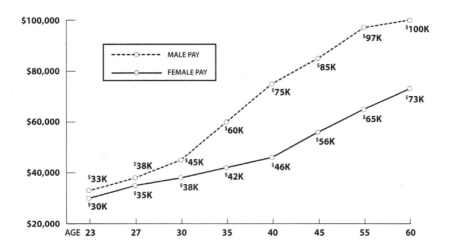

In this example, both the young man, indicated by the dotted line, and the young woman, indicated by the solid line, begin their first jobs right out of college, at the age of twenty-three.

Both lines indicate their respective salaries increasing in a linear progression. Notice that his salary starts at $33,000, while hers begins at $30,000. This was because he negotiated his starting rate, while she accepted the initial offer without a counter. Both professionals do the same work and remain with the same company until they reach age fifty-five. They hold the same jobs at the time of retirement. Notice that his final pay is nearly $100,000 a year, while she has yet to achieve $75,000. This is an extreme example of male/female pay variances over a career—or is it? (Answer: It's not!)

FACTORS

I'm not blind to the many other factors in play here. I understand the impact of additional education and certifications, not to mention the "good old boy" network. I'm aware of the impact of a woman's childbearing years and the sacrifices of stay-at-home moms who lose career years. But we all know the dynamics are shifting, especially since women are obtaining college degrees at a higher rate than men.

If you haven't figured it out by now, I'm all for *equal pay for equal work* and more, the *proper pay for the best performance.* The boost to the economy alone of paying women appropriately (and anyone else similarly discriminated against) would be phenomenal!

Moms and dads, I implore you to teach your daughters to hold out for an increase in pay at their first professional negotiation. Done early in a career, the financial impact and what it stands for can be life changing. Teach them Nettie's fallback negotiation tactic. Teach your young women that they have the option to say no and hold out for a better offer or to seek employment elsewhere.

And guys, to be fair, major successes deserve promotion. But I also know having access to the boss on the golf course and over drinks, access which your female colleagues may not have, provides men with an unjust advantage.

Q-STUDY NO. 9

Ellie: Process Improvement
"Most people have a hard time believing it."

Process improvement, in its simplest form, is about analyzing a company's existing practices and recommending improvements. Ellie is an independent project manager (not a full-time employee) who specializes in improving processes and practices, among other things.

The company that engaged her, one of the well-known names in the industrial equipment services industry, had recently acquired another company. Ellie received a sixty-day contract to go in and do what she does, which is to make things better.

Here is how Ellie tells it:

> Before the project, there was no production planning in the product finishing area, nor was there any organization. Personnel would often spend hours just hunting for the right product to finish. The [on-site] equipment wasn't capable of handling newer products, so setup time was extensive, which limited the quantities of materials that could be finished at one time. Needless to say, it was a significant product bottleneck. Also, because the equipment was outdated and not user-friendly, there were quite a number of products that had to be refinished because of quality issues.

> After I completed the project, the team had new processes for receiving goods finished by type, order, and final finish style. They also had the ability to finish greater quantities of products at once, drastically increasing the amount of product to be worked on. As a bonus, quality issues also dropped to nearly zero.

Ellie told me that after her recommended processes were implemented, production rose from 165 units to 694 per week—an increase of 420%!

Since Ellie was on-site for only a short period, we can only measure what she was able to substantiate while there. The company most likely saw other cost reductions, and though some, like shipping, would have risen—which is a good problem—this is not something she can evaluate unless she were to do a follow-up consultation.

For this illustration, Ellie knew there was a profit of $3,000 per delivered unit. This was the number that was in place at the time Ellie arrived on-site. Based on this and increased weekly production, we can determine Ellie's QTNT score for this project.

(A) Enhanced production: 694 units x $3,000 profit each = $2,082,000
(B) Previous production: 165 units x $3,000 profit each = $495,000
Revenue increase (A - B): $2,082,000 - $495,000 = $1,587,000
$1,587,000 represents new, additional revenue per week.

Ellie was paid just shy of $8,000 per month, and since the numbers above represent one week of productivity only, I will use one week of Ellie's pay, or $2,000, to calculate her Quotient.

$$\frac{\text{Weekly manufacturing revenue increase} \ = \$1,587,000}{\text{Ellie's pay for one week} \ = \$2,000}$$

Ellie's QTNT score for one week (only) of this 60-day project = 793.5

As you already know, this Q-Study does not take into account the cost of overhead, so the Quotient above is overly generous. Ellie was working on contract, and this was all the information she was provided while on the job.

There is no question that this is a monumental Quotient! But it happens. I have seen it many, many times.

I'll let Ellie close out this example in her own words:

I have more accomplishments from that year, totaling in the multimillions [of dollars]. Honestly, most people have a hard time believing it. You see, improving things is what I did for a living! Projects like this were a constant story.

21

The Quotient and the Future of Employment

I N CASE YOU haven't been paying attention for the last couple of decades or more, we are currently witnessing a complete overhaul of how we work. The inescapable fact is contract employment is becoming the norm rather than traditional, full-time, long-term employment. Fewer full-time employees are making it to their company's retirement finish line. This situation can be, for lack of a better word, *managed* somewhat with the Quotient. However, every person reading this book can anticipate getting the boot when they begin to cost their company more than it costs to keep them on staff. (You will find an eye-opening discussion on this topic in chapter 23, "The Earning Curve.")

Freelance. Temp. Gig. Contract. Call it what you will, I can assure you this kind of work arrangement is becoming the standard at all levels of employment in companies large and small. Many positions that were staffed with full-time workers not so long ago are now being designated "contract" or "project" (a term that has come to be used interchangeably with *contract* in some industries). Or these jobs are being contracted out to staffing or outsourcing firms who then supply long-term—you guessed it—contract workers. There is a justifiable reason for why this is happening, and it all comes down to money. Simply stated, employers cannot continue to fund thirty-five-year-plus retirements.

THE RETIREMENT PENDULUM SWINGS BACK

Before World War II, unless you worked for the federal government (the civil service), it's unlikely you received any benefits from your private employer beyond a ham at Christmas. The average wage earner worked hard, saved hard, and planned for his and his spouse's "golden years."

(The workforce at that time consisting mostly of men.) Families lived closer together and tended to look after each other.

Post–World War II America was a new place with grand opportunities. Homes were being built by the thousands, and, as a result, the extended family began to disintegrate as their members moved farther away from each other. After acquiring a new car (necessary to reach the 'burbs), members of households lusted after the latest appliances and amenities. America saw that all of this was good, but manufacturers, especially the automobile companies, had a severe problem.

Over sixteen million Americans—again, mostly men—served during the war. Of those, some 415,000 did not return. Sprint forward to 1948 or so, and this catastrophic loss of working-age manpower led to a shortage of workers when US manufacturing desperately needed them. Companies began to offer incentives to attract (and steal) employees. Thus, retirement and other benefits, as we now know them, were invented. Manufacturing became one of the best jobs in the land, based not just on wages but also on the perks!

Before and after World War II, workers retired at about fifty-five years of age when the average life expectancy for a male was sixty-one years. Based on this statistic, companies figured they would be on the hook to pay benefits for just a few "affordable" years. Today, that same male can be expected to live over seventy-six years, and women, who began actively moving into the workforce in the 1960s and '70s, live even longer. What was a great way to attract workers in the 1940s and '50s now keeps compensation and benefits managers, CFOs, and CEOs awake at night. Today, people who have worked thirty years for a company can potentially receive benefits for more years than they spent on the job. As you can see, the pendulum has indeed swung back.

The future of the corporate workforce, beyond those workers required to manage the core day-to-day operations, such as finance, accounting, legal, and management, will be one of short- and long-term temporary workers or contractors who do not receive benefits and will be required to work hard, save hard, and make their own plans for retirement.

The takeaway here is, if you work for anyone, you have no choice but to speak up for yourself on my previously mentioned irregular-regular basis. This may sound dire, but it doesn't have to be. With your knowledge of the Quotient, your measurable contributions will take you a long way down the road, to the time when you can decide to quit working on your own terms.

22 The (Employment) Circle of Life

A S WITH LIFE, there is a birth, growth, maturity, and waning pattern to employment. Calculating your Quotient throughout your professional life will be beneficial to you up until the last day of your career. Let me explain.

A new graduate enters the workforce. This young person is out to make a name for himself. He is hired, goes to work, and straightaway sets his sights, whether consciously or not, on taking over his boss's job. This is normal and necessary for the health and well-being of the organization. His manager now has a potential future adversary or a protégé, and only time will tell which it will be.

In retrospect, this was the same mindset the current manager had when she was starting out. It's the law of the jungle: every person is on his or her own, and only the fittest will survive. And while this is taking place on the workers' side of the command structure, the same promotion-seeking game is being played out on the management side of the house.

And so it goes. Invariably things work themselves out, and life carries on. New players come along to take up new positions, the weak move on, and the vaunted move up.

DISCRIMINATION

There is, and always will be, some kind of discrimination that will play a role in this "life and death" saga. I firmly believe that no matter what you look like or how different you may be, if you can *make a company money* or *save them money* and can *express* that you did so, you can get the job, earn the promotion, or retain your position.

But I'm not saying it's easy or that discrimination is not a factor.

There will always be employers/managers/coworkers who outright disregard the fundamentals of civility or won't even acknowledge equal employment opportunity laws.

That said, this is as good a place as any to begin talking about the difference between age discrimination and being aged out based on declining performance and how the Quotient impacts this discussion. I have told my audiences for years that the one fact of life (and employment) no one can avoid is you will be old much longer than you will be young. So it can't hurt anybody, at any age, to begin thinking about on-the-job age issues.

But in the end, it is my "make them money or save them money" mantra that carries the day. The Quotient accordingly reflects this.

ON AGE

Take my word for it: everyone will at some point suffer age-related discrimination on the job (and off). But do not confuse age discrimination with termination as a result of declining performance, or aging out.

Unfortunately, and not always improperly, it is very easy for management to decide they can replace sixty-year-old Keith, who makes $145,000 a year plus bonuses, with twenty-nine-year-old Jennifer, who has an MBA and is currently earning $75,000 a year. (To be clear, I'm not faulting go-getter Jennifer for landing the job! Good for her!) Bear in mind, always, that a company is a living, breathing organism that will do what it must in order to survive.

This concept might also take you back to the discussion we had in chapter 8, "Your Commercial Value." That viewpoint states you are only worth what the market is willing to pay for your talents, skills, or services today. The QTNT PVC is the tool that can keep you in, and ahead of, the game.

HOW TO AVOID CAREER DEATH

What if, toward the end of your circle of life—er, employment journey—you do not have to "die prematurely" (be terminated, get the ax, be put out to pasture, etc.)?

The reality is the number of workers who retire on their own terms today is growing smaller. Once a company has determined that certain team members are no longer able to deliver relevant value, there is no reason for the company to continue to pay them. This isn't personal. It's business. Big bucks require the corresponding delivery of big value. Until the day you retire or can leave on your own terms, you cannot—I repeat, cannot—take a break from promoting yourself.

Knowing your QTNT score is certainly not a guarantee you will never be terminated, but doing a few calculations while on the corporate roller coaster will go a long way toward keeping you on your toes and prepped to fight the good fight if ever you find yourself in that situation. Keep your Accomplishments Inventory current, including the economic value of those achievements.

FENDING OFF THE NEXT GENERATION, NO MATTER YOUR AGE

Both men and women must remember there will come a time when you can expect to have to fend off the next generation. This is not a bad thing. It is, after all, that circle of life. They are right behind you. You know them. You do not want to be at the top of your game, thinking it can't happen to you, when out of the blue you are out on the street, never having seen what hit you. (I have seen this occur so many times I have gotten pretty good at predicting it to my employed clientele.)

This slow-motion tussle develops over time. My best advice is to keep your eyes open and always, on a moment's notice, be able to express a recent contribution in a way that speaks to your current value. This is that accomplishments mindset I mention so often. Watch how your sales staff talk about their latest successes. Remember, this is not bragging. Get comfortable with talking about yourself. To paraphrase the old Hollywood adage, "You're only as good as your last accomplishment."

* * *

In the next chapter, I make the eye-opening counterclaim that most age-related terminations, perceived as discriminatory, are not. (*That* should get some people riled!) See if you don't agree with me that both of my positions on this topic are reasonable.

23 The Earning Curve™

BILL, A SENIOR manager, has been with his company more than thirty years. Recently, Bill read this book and took the concepts in it to heart, and at the age of fifty-eight, decided to begin keeping a tally of his weekly accomplishments. Wisely, he also decided to graph his entire career Quotient-style.

Bill has a corner office and a great compensation package, but his QTNT score indicates he is not in near as good a shape, career-wise, as he thought he was based on what he is paid. Even worse, he hasn't been for some time. Why have they kept him around? Contacts? Industry knowledge? Expertise? Whatever the reason, he now realizes it can't last much longer.

Bill's Quotient history, below, and the accompanying graph illustrate the biggest issue: Since the age of forty-five, his performance has been declining in a downward curve. After peaking at $265,000, Bill has never again produced that much money for the company.

Here is Bill's Quotient history:

Bill's Career QTNT Calculations

Age	Contribution	÷	Salary	=	Score
25	$55,000	÷	$20,000	=	2.75
30	$85,000	÷	$40,000	=	2.125
35	$210,000	÷	$60,000	=	3.5
40	$240,000	÷	$80,000	=	3.0
45	$265,000	÷	$100,000	=	2.65
50	$175,000	÷	$125,000	=	1.4

Age	Contribution	÷	Salary	=	Score
53	$120,000	÷	$145,000	=	0.83
58	$100,000	÷	$155,000	=	0.65

BILL'S CAREER EARNING CURVE

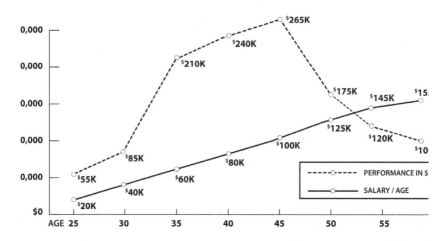

The upper dotted line indicates Bill's performance in dollars. Note that Bill's production peaked at age forty-five. The solid line angling upward from left to right indicates his salary.

Bill can now see how his performance has diminished over time while his pay has continued to rise. This is not good.

As the curve turns downward, there comes the point when, at age fifty-three, Bill's production of $120,000 is $25,000 *less* than his annual pay. You can also see that Bill hit this slide in production after peaking at $265,000 some eight years earlier.

This scenario is not uncommon. Bill had come to a point in his career where he thought he "had it made" and allowed complacency to set in. As I have said before, you can never quit promoting yourself—but first, you have to have a reason to do so. Honestly, termination is eminent for Bill—and notice that the reason would *not* be age but rather lack of performance. Are there options? Maybe.

- He could start working harder to improve his value to the company, which is a no-brainer, but he no longer has the runway to get this done.

- He could take voluntary early retirement.

- Alternatively, because Bill now knows his historical Quotient scores, he can devise a plan and approach his boss (and human resources) to preempt the end-of-the-world discussion that he knows is coming.

In his plan, Bill will offer to reduce his salary, hopefully retaining enough to continue to support his family after some belt tightening. He will ask to keep his health insurance and other benefits in place. At the same time, he will propose a three-year plan whereby he will focus on value contribution while aggressively sharing his industry knowledge with the next generation.

The benefit of this plan to the company is that they minimize brain drain. (How many times have companies had to reach out to former employees and contract them at a higher rate to get them back in the huddle?) Ultimately, Bill may be able to negotiate a retirement date some time into the future. But the reality remains that, as his production has decreased, he is no longer in the driver's seat.

* * *

Regarding my counterpoint close to the previous chapter, and founded on my own client-based experience, I stand by my earlier statement that many, if not most, perceived age-related terminations are not discriminatory but are more often due to a lack of measurable delivery of value by the employee. If the reason is lack of production, as you already know, the Quotient will point that out.

Q-STUDY NO. 10

Peter: Executive VP, Cybersecurity
"Change Leadership and Sales Management"

I am quoting this study exactly as the client submitted it for my review when we worked together. The product was an enterprise-level anti-virus software product.

EXCELLENCE IN CHANGE MANAGEMENT

Strength: *Strategic contributor who competently takes the lead in conceptualizing and executing the changes required to drive growth, improve operational performance, and optimize processes. Results: Increased value to the company and customer.*

Challenge: *Replace a legacy of organizational misdirection, poor competitive positioning, and incorrect go-to-market strategies with an organizational structure, sales model, and culture that would enable successful sales execution within the small and medium business (SMB) and enterprise IT security markets.*

Action: *Planned and executed a multiphased implementation to restructure the sales teams; streamlined and shortened the sales process by using consistent, structured pipeline management methods during initial contact, lead generation, demonstration, and purchasing phases. Formed a well-targeted, unique offering specific to the vertical market being pursued.*

Result: *Put the company on a growth curve and success path by creating a highly structured and reproducible customer engagement system that leveraged one brand and a single-vision management team. Shortened the sales cycle by eight months, increased the average new customer seat licenses purchased by 423% (from 120 to 628), and achieved a 525% increase in the average order size within one year, from $5,290 to $33,100.*

After reading this, you would not be surprised to know Peter went on to become the COO for a company in the cybersecurity field.

As you probably understand from reading other Q-Studies, this accomplishment was only one of several prepared for me by Peter when we were working together. I know this personal achievement took place over two and a half years, that the exact gross sales for this security product during this time was $25,143,001.43, and that his pay at the time was $450,000 annually. We now have enough information to calculate Peter's QTNT score.

First we need to determine Peter's total pay received during his two and a half years on the job.

$$\$450,000 \div 12 = \$37,500 \text{ per month}$$
$$\$37,500 \times 30 \text{ months (2.5 years)} = \$1,125,000$$

or

$$\$450,000 \times 2.5 \text{ years} = \$1,125,000$$

Let's calculate:

$$\frac{\$25,143,000 \text{ (total sales over 2.5 years)}}{\$1,125,000 \text{ (total compensation)}} = 22.34$$

Peter's QTNT score for his effort was more than 22 times what he was paid to deliver this value.

What I genuinely appreciate about Peter's presentation statement—and this is one every sales professional should review closely—are the details. I like the Strength, Challenge, Action, and Result headers better than the more widely used STAR (Situation, Task, Action, Result). Every accomplishment he provided to me was presented in exactly this format. Don't you think an employer—at any level—would appreciate the breakdown of effort followed up with a concise explanation of the results? Imagine showing up with your list of accomplishments, each broken down similarly, at your next performance review.

24 Personal Performance Appraisal: Identifying Your Value

J
UST ABOUT ANY job you can name in the known universe has a set of key performance indicators (KPIs) ascribed to it that can be thought of as minimum or perhaps ideal performance targets. KPIs are used throughout most organizations and at all levels. Does the performance information your company provides you give you enough data to determine your Quotient? Can you divide your rate of pay into any numerical data provided to you? (Note that even if you do have such information available to you, it may or may not be relevant to your unique, over-and-above-the-call-of-duty accomplishments. You will still have to identify and quantify those on your own.)

MAXIMIZING YOUR PERFORMANCE APPRAISAL

Navigating the subjectivity of the current appraisal system by which you may have to live and die, as well as the necessary rigidity of KPIs, the question then becomes: How can you best utilize what you know about your accomplishments and the corresponding QTNT Personal Value Contribution score for each, and be able to *objectively* express your value to the company? The point here is not just to maximize your performance appraisal but also to add your voice to the discussion. In other words, I want your review to be conducted on a two-way street with your participation being "more equal" than your supervisor's.

Those KPIs assigned to you are mandatory and need to be your first priority. But for your extra-professional well-being, the Quotient is meant to help you notice when you do your regular work impressively well and to promote the extraordinary accomplishments your supervisors never see. Of course, some of this has to do with proximity and access to your boss, but even then, you are not your boss's only direct report or responsibility, right?

Your plan of action is to meet the minimums (plus) required of you and be prepared to discuss, based on your Personal Value Calculations, how you exceeded those minimums. As I have tried to express in the Q-Studies, be creative. Try to observe what you do from an owner's perspective. I hope you have found common ground in those examples and can emulate the way we obtained those values.

If you have access to the same operating cost information your supervisor has, describe your performance and quantify the value of your contributions in terms of savings or revenue generated. As you do this, speak in terms your boss would use.

Next, explain how you added up that value and divided the total by your pay and came up with your scores. Now you can share how the value you recently delivered is X times more than your rate of pay.

In the event you don't have access to cost/expense figures, do the best with what you have. Many of the Q-Studies offer fairly simple workarounds that may assist you in establishing valuations. Doing so on your own shows management you are proactively looking more deeply at things, including your contributions. As you explain the QTNT PVC process, your supervisor may be willing to share actuals instead of the workarounds you used to determine your values. Assuming your boss has never heard of the Quotient, there's a good chance he or she will be interested in knowing more about it. There is never a better time than a review to introduce your boss to the process.

NEVER ASSUME

On a different note, do not assume your immediate supervisor knows *how* to conduct a performance review or will do you justice—at least, from your point of view. This is not uncommon, especially with new managers. Let's face it: regardless of training and instructions, appraisals are hard to do, and no amount of training will take the subjectivity out of the current process.

You, on the other hand, are heading into your review with a goal in mind, and that should be, at a minimum, a raise. What you *don't* want at the end of this meeting is a pat on the back and a keep-up-the-good-work handshake from your supervisor. What you *do* want is to see that surprised expression that indicates your boss had no idea just how much you contribute to the bottom line. This is an important aspect of how you talk yourself up in your review, especially if you work with a team or are one of several people who do similar work for your company, division, or branch. And once again, I repeat: This review is not about the team. It is about *you*.

Your immediate supervisor may or may not have the authority to determine the size of your raise, award you a bonus, or promote you. Nevertheless, as this is the place where those discussions about pay and promotion begin, they continue with others up the food chain. Your goal is to have your importance to the company validated and documented in such a way that makes people notice, even if you have to do the documenting yourself.

25 Speaking Up at Your Appraisal

THERE ARE BOOKS and videos of all manner that talk about preparing and presenting yourself for a performance appraisal, so I won't spend a whole lot of time on this topic. However, beyond your QTNT PVC score(s), I do have a shortlist of some considerations that may benefit you.

- **Initiative:** If you are the kind of person who is not afraid to step up and take charge of a situation, then you should also have no problem taking the *initiative* and speaking up for yourself regarding this specific quality. Never assume your boss knows exactly what you do—especially if you are a quiet performer.

- **Comparison between you and your coworkers:** You don't have to "bad mouth" anyone, but do speak to how you offer more in terms of contribution either in revenue or in savings.

- **Comparison between you and the market:** Be prepared to speak to your value compared to similarly skilled professionals. Express why you are the person whose performance exceeds that of anyone else who could be brought in from off the street.

- **Salary research:** Know how your rate of pay compares with others who do what you do. You can find this information at BLS.gov (Search for "wage data by area and occupation") or Salary.com. Also, I am always impressed with the depth and breadth of the Robert Half Salary Guide and Calculator at RobertHalf.com.

- **Cost of your employment:** Know how much it costs to keep you on the job. I'm talking about such things as pay, perks, benefits, bonuses, and any other contributions the company may offer to keep you on the payroll. Knowing overhead costs for elements such as facilities, equipment, and training will impress your bosses. Not sure how to find this information? Start by asking your immediate supervisor. Someone not too far up the line has this information and is most likely willing to share.

- **Contributions:** Do not be shy about speaking to your efficiency, education, leadership skills, and other attributes as well as your ability to get along with others in the company. Soft skills are valuable to an employer.

- **Cost-benefit analysis:** This is what the Quotient is all about. If your company knows the QTNT Personal Value Calculation, expect to be dealing with it in your appraisal. If not, be prepared to speak in Quotient-based multiples. For example: "I contributed value equal to nine times my rate of pay to the organization this past year." Then be able to show how you came to that conclusion.

- **Your future employment:** Talk about the company's mission and goals and where you fit into the plan, their hierarchy, and the future.

Nick: Chief Technology Officer
"Healthcare Acquisition and Integration"

When Nick and I first met, he was seeking a chief information officer position (CIO). He was more than qualified for the position, but the problem lay, as is the case in any interview, in how well he would be able to tell the various stories of his achievements. And he had a bunch of them.

When working with clients, as you know, I prefer they provide a long-form, written history of each accomplishment that includes the what, where, when, why, and how behind each achievement. (You will remember I don't need the "who" in this description. The "who" is *always* you!)

Nick has the unique ability to keep his accounts exceptionally brief while providing all the details key to understanding what he accomplished. Below is one of those descriptions. I'll follow on the other side with a QTNT PVC. (All company names have been changed to generic descriptions representing their positions in this transaction.)

Medical Group 1's (MG1) growth strategy included aggressive membership expansion in the South. Expansion was to include the acquisition of a small, troubled health plan, Medical Group 2 (MG2), in the area. MG2 included sixty thousand Medicare Advantage, Medicaid, and Rx members. The strategy was to acquire the health plan, integrate the Medicare members, and divest the Medicaid and Rx business. I was responsible for information technology as the interim CIO as well as overseeing the integration and divestitures. Budget reductions of 50% and a fully implemented strategy were to be achieved in eight months. Plan execution began April 1 and was completed December 10 with all targets met.

MG2 was acquired, and the Medicare Advantage members were integrated into MG1. This integration and the divestiture of two business segments were achieved in eight months, on schedule and within budget, saving $3,700,000 annually in IT costs. In addition, an organizational membership expansion of fifty thousand lives was realized.

Told you that would be brief! But all the details are there except for Nick's salary, which at the time was $175,000. Since we have no way of determining the value of the expansion of fifty thousand additional customers, we can't add that to his Quotient score. Too bad. There was a lot of "newfound" money there!

Here is Nick's QTNT PVC:

$$\frac{\$3{,}700{,}000 \text{ in IT and organizational savings achieved}}{\$175{,}000 \text{ salary}} = 21.1$$

As you can see, I am treating this eight-month project as if it took an entire year. Let's do this same calculation based on eight months instead.

Nick's annual salary was $175,000, which we can divide by 12 to get his monthly rate of $14,583.33 x 8 months = $116,666.64.

This calculation will provide an even higher Quotient for Nick:

$$\frac{\$3{,}700{,}000}{\$116{,}700} = 31.7$$

In this case, breaking down Nick's annual salary into a monthly rate of pay gave him a ten-point increase in his QTNT score, to 31.7. Significant!

26
There Is No I in Team

WHAT IF ONE of your more significant accomplishments was a team effort? What if it took eight of you to _____? How do you express *team* in your Accomplishments Statement when I have been telling you that the "who" in your statement is always you? The simple answer is you don't.

EXPRESSING TEAM ACCOMPLISHMENTS IN THE SINGULAR

Recruiters will tell you that, although you worked with a team, you must point out your specific contributions to the success of the overall project as if you had done the deal by yourself. This is correct. Although teams do get reviewed, that is not what we are talking about here. This can be hard sometimes. You may not be comfortable focusing only on yourself, but any raise or promotion is not going to the team—it is going to you. Or, rather, it will when you know how to express your contribution in a singular manner. But shouldn't credit always be given where credit is due? Yes, except for now. Seriously. Never feel bad about promoting only yourself. Here is an example of a team member's contribution written in the voice of one person:

> *Responsible for achieving 97% occupancy of the Acme Tower due to the diligent and consistent pursuit of a competing property's primary tenants. Relocated five tenants this year for a total of 120,000 net rentable square feet leased, resulting in $2,760,000 new gross annual revenue.*

I'm certain you realize that no real estate deal is a solo achievement. It takes many people moving in the same direction, even if there were several leasing agents working in concert to accomplish the negotiation, renovation of space, and relocation of new tenants. Nevertheless, nowhere in my description of this achievement did I say or even imply that a team of any kind was involved. To someone in the industry, there would be an unwritten understanding that you did not accomplish this all on your own. Nevertheless, to state an accomplishment in this manner is normal and acceptable.

Note: The Quotient is also an ideal tool for measuring the contributions of teams, departments, branches, et cetera.

27 Personal Performance Review: The Work Diary

THE RESULTS OF your performance appraisal(s) directly impact your chances of advancement and your quality of life. That's a given. This is probably truer in large organizations than in small ones. Should you remain with the same company for many years or your entire career, these reports taken all together could make the difference between promotion into senior management or not. That's how it's done in the military.

CREATING A WORK DIARY FROM YOUR APPOINTMENT CALENDAR

It is for this reason I recommend that people should keep a professional diary of the things they do at work as they do them—ideally at the end of each day. This is about enhancing that performance mindset. By memorializing them, you reinforce those things you want remembered for when the moment to share happens. Pay attention to what you are doing as you do it. The trick is to become disciplined at this.

But wait a minute; you're busy, on the run, under the gun, on the clock, pressed for time right now, right? It's pretty easy to be executing great work and not make note of it. I have personally had occasion to be talking with someone and suddenly find myself reflecting on something I had done that was pretty remarkable even though I hadn't thought of it as such at the time. You probably have had that experience too, especially now that I have you thinking about past performance. Remember that time when you knocked it out of the park because you _____?

All this memorializing of events entails is taking five minutes at the end of each day to annotate your appointment calendar with what you did. After that, on occasion scroll back to see what you did and when. Note that I said "what you did" instead of "what you *accomplished*," because you are not toting up wins. Not yet.

TWO REASONS TO CREATE A WORK DIARY

A week from now you won't remember those things you did today that could be the start of something great. I mean, think about it: You can't tell me what you had for lunch today, but you think you'll remember that remarkable little incident at work last Tuesday that had some snap? Not likely!

Second, it is reasonable to assume that at some point in time you will have cause to identify those simple benchmarks such as dates or events when you began a specific project and continued to move forward with it. Nobody can argue with you when you can show them that you began the X project in May of last year.

When you first begin keeping this calendar/diary, it may not amount to much. Unless you land a multimillion-dollar deal tomorrow, there will be days when you just won't feel like you have accomplished a darn thing. But that's not how achievements happen. They materialize over time.

I have to tell you, it's pretty satisfying to look back over your recent history and see that on the first of July you got the approval to launch the marketing campaign that went live on July 23. Scrolling forward, you see that on August 1 the program went viral and to date has generated $7,231,955 in new revenue. Would you have been able to anticipate this kind of success a month ago? This aspect of calendaring and the value you gain from it will make more and more sense to you as you begin to work the process. From the Quotient point of view, this is a habit to embrace.

> **SIDENOTE**: Did you know you can copy and paste complete emails into the day/dates on your calendar? This is a great way to keep all pertinent information in one place.

Q-STUDY NO. 12

Allen: Construction/ Bridge Building

"Saving Minutes and Thousands of Dollars"

You met Allen in Q-Study No. 6 and learned about two foundations that were poured under his supervision. Well, he's back, and the reason I share his next accomplishment with you is because I want you to recognize how tiny, incremental amounts of time (or materials or inventory or whatever you work with) may appear insignificant but when added up can cost—or save—your company a lot of money. There is a good chance this study will help you look a little closer at what you do. Every little bit really does count. Maybe you should be counting that stuff you work with and begin reaping the benefit.

In Allen's previous study, "The Cement Pour," the two massive slabs of concrete his team poured were 6 feet tall by 20 feet wide by 120 feet long. This pour created two huge structures that were now physically in the way! To get to their daily work locations, some twelve hundred workers spent five to ten minutes every day making the trek one way just to get to work. Once again, to provide conservative results, we will base the following calculations on one thousand workers, the same as we did in Allen's previous example.

Already having the necessary materials and skilled labor on-site, Allen, without seeking management approval (sometimes it's easier to beg forgiveness than to ask for permission), decided to design and erect a temporary bridge that spanned those gigantic cement slabs—at virtually no cost to the company. Imagine the savings that could be realized by getting his workers to the job more quickly, even if by only five minutes a day.

Using nothing more than the power of observation, Allen saw that his crews were making several one-way trips daily on the clock: one outbound in the morning, two out and back for the midmorning break, two out and back for lunch, and two for the midafternoon break—a total of seven trips. (We won't include the return trip at the end of the day because, presumably, they were off the clock.)

We already know Allen's pay rate from the previous example ($45.67/hour). He said it took each worker five to ten minutes to get to the job site, so, of course, we will use the conservative, shorter time factor. Let's do the math.

5 minutes x 1,000 workers x 7 trips = 35,000 minutes
35,000 minutes ÷ 60 minutes = 583 lost hours of production per day
(The company was getting nothing in return for those paid hours.)

We know the average pay for these workers was $40 per hour.

583 hours x $40 = $23,320 per day
This is the cost to the company of 1,000 workers taking the round-about way to their job site *daily* before the bridge was erected.

Allen told me this part of the overall project took a total of five months from start to finish. I do not know how long the bridge was in place, so for our purposes, we'll agree that the bridge was in place for ninety work days.

$23,320 x 90 days = $2,098,800 saved in wages
(*in 5-minute increments!*) over 90 days

To determine Allen's Quotient for this single project, use his previously calculated hourly pay.

90 days x 8 hours per day x $45.67 per hour = $32,882.40 =
Allen's pay for this period of time

Total saved by installing crossover bridge = $2,098,800
Allen's pay for this period of time = $32,882.40

Allen's QTNT PVC for taking the initiative to build this bridge = 63.83

Allen returned a value to his organization of 63 times
his hourly pay totaled over 90 workdays.

* * *

What you have just seen is the second of two measurable accomplishments valued on the only information at hand: wages. Once again, had all enterprise costs been included, these Quotient scores would have been significantly different, much lower in fact. But both Quotients (in Q-Study No. 6 and this one) were calculated with the best information Allen had at hand.

Depending on your line of work, this might be the best model for you to consider when scoring your Quotient, especially if you work on a contract or project basis.

28 Calculating Your Annual Quotient (Including Q = 1)

YOU WILL NOTICE that in each Q-Study I provided a QTNT PVC score for *that specific event* only. Those examples may have been calculated in weeks, days, or hours, but at year-end you need to be able to compile your Quotient scores in a manner that reflects the sum total of the various contributions you made to your company over the previous year. It's time to show you how to compile multiple PVCs into a single *annual* Quotient.

Allen's two case studies offer up the perfect scenario for me to illustrate how to calculate your annual score. To do so we will assume Allen's work was accomplished within a single fiscal year.

The first value to be considered for Allen's annual QTNT score is the one he is *required* to achieve just to keep his job: his Q = 1. For our purposes we will assume he has met the requirements to justify his annual salary of $95,000. You can see his Q = 1 as item #1 in the calculation below.

Q-STUDY NO. 6: THE CEMENT POUR

Next, let's look at Allen's Quotient score in Q-Study No. 6. Note that his PVC for that *single* event was 154.56, but this was based on an *hourly*, not annual, rate of pay for his work on the foundation pour. Now we will add the *value* (savings) *only* of that single accomplishment to his Q = 1 value of $95,000. Note: Do not make the mistake of adding the Quotient *score* that he achieved for that accomplishment. Focus on the dollars saved only.

Allen is able to make a defensible claim that he saved the company $480,000 in worker pay by completing the second foundation pour in

30% less time than it took to complete the first pour. This is based on the fact that we were only able to calculate savings based on the hours worked and the hourly rate of pay for his staff of one thousand. We will add this number to his Q = 1 value. See item #2 below.

Q-STUDY NO. 12: BRIDGE BUILDING

By erecting a span to bridge the two foundations that resulted from the cement pours above, Allen was able to save his company over $2,000,000 by eliminating a significant number of the minutes his one thousand workers were wasting walking the job site. For our purposes here, once again, we will only focus on the savings Allen achieved and add that to our two other data points. See item #3 below.

1. Allen's base pay value (Q = 1):	**$ 95,000**
2. Documented savings (Q-Study No. 6):	+ $ 480,000
3. Documented savings (Q-Study No. 12):	+ $ 2,098,800
Total value Allen delivered his company this year	= **$ 2,673,800**

Based on the savings calculated in his two Q-Studies plus his required Q = 1 valuation, the total of Allen's contributions to his employer this year comes to $2,673,800. In order to determine his annual Quotient, we will now divide that total by his *annual* rate of pay, his Q = 1, of $95,000.

Total annual value contribution	=	$ 2,673,800
Allen's base pay	=	$ 95,000
Allen's annual QTNT score	=	28.15

Whether based on his per-event Quotients or his calculated annual score, Allen continues to prove he is an exceptionally valuable employee to his organization.

THE Q = 1 TAKEAWAY

The most important takeaway from this chapter is for you to understand that, as an employee who has been on the job for more than a year, you are most likely achieving your Q = 1 or you would not still be on the payroll.

This number, your base salary (never to be confused with your net, or take-home, pay), will *always* be the first numerical factor you will add to your other achievement values to determine your annual Quotient rating.

Furthermore, your Q = 1 (that same base-pay figure) will *always* be the divisor, that is, the number that will be divided into the total cumulative value of your accomplishments for the purpose of producing your annual Quotient score.

This is worth repeating: Your Q = 1 (base pay) will always be the first value used to determine your annual PVC. As well, your Q = 1 will always be the number you will divide into the total value of your contributions to obtain your annual Quotient.

29 Personal Performance Appraisal Prep

WELCOME TO YOUR annual performance appraisal preparation, where I make the case that any achievement worth presenting to management is worth examination. You only get one shot at this, after all. Think it over. Think it through. Ask others what they recall of your performance this year. When recollecting accomplishments, write down every point you can think of: the good, the bad, and the ugly (the bad and the ugly will remind you of how you improved them). Plan on telling a story. Be prepared to provide all the details you might expect someone in charge to want to know. A great way to set up the story is by starting with the problem you encountered.

After twelve Q-Studies (there are two more coming up), you now know what a professional accomplishment presentation should look and sound like. Recognize that knowing your Quotient for any one of your accomplishments provides a firm foundation from which to point out to management that you are the next person in line for promotion.

WHAT, WHERE, WHEN, WHY, AND HOW

Start with the what, where, when, why, and how (WWWWH) of the project. (Remember, you are the who.) When you can answer WWW-WH for each accomplishment, you are 99% ready to present. The last thing, the punch line to each story, will be the net results realized by the company.

Always be thinking in terms of this punch line. As you write, think of each achievement on your list as a short, freestanding article. Every story needs a beginning, a middle, and an end. The end will always be the WOW!

This list, or exercise, is *about* you but not *for* you. It is for your supervisors. Note that that last word is plural. Keep your audience in mind.

- Ponder the details as if you were an employer. It is every employer's dream to hire people who think like an owner. Ask yourself: How will a senior member of the management team accept this statement from his or her point of view? Did this achievement hit (or exceed) goals and show consistency of performance? Will your supervisor(s) view your statements as producing value in comparison to what you are being paid?

- The types of situations you encountered and how you dealt with them are a core principle of presenting valuable accomplishments. Without problems, who needs you, right? Problems create opportunities. (Remember "bad" and "ugly" above?) Think hard and deep about difficulties that someone without your specific skills and expertise would not have been able to overcome.

- Was the project completed on time and on budget? If so, share those details. If not, be ready to explain why not.

- Did a team member or members not perform as expected? How did you handle the situation? You don't have to name names, but this sort of issue is an ideal one for you to point out your managerial skills. Some of your greatest accomplishments could be based on your having taken over the reins of an existing project to restage it.

As you make notes and flesh out your accomplishments, go for the wow factor whenever possible. Illustrate how you stand head and shoulders above the crowd.

When composing an accomplishment, your goal is to make yourself more compelling and more memorable than any of your coworkers. You will be leaving this document behind. Revise it until you get it right.

30 Personal Performance Appraisal: A Revolution

THERE IS A revolution coming, and it is rooted in the elimination of the performance appraisal/management review as we know it. This revolution will alter the current focus on subjective performance appraisal by including the objective Quotient-based evaluation as a free-standing appraisal or as an add-on to current subjective platforms. In the event your organization decides to adopt the Quotient as a standard for appraisal, it could be entirely up to you, the individual, to produce your assessment.

Many well-known companies have already done away with the traditional review and replaced it with appraisals of their own design. There will always be a need for employees to be measured and rated, but shouldn't an accurate measurement of an individual's *contribution* to the organization be the foremost indicator of an employee's value?

THE GOOD AND THE BAD ABOUT CURRENT REVIEWS

Let me tell you what is good about employee performance reviews as we currently know them. They are subjective, meaning that your boss, the person who knows you and your work product best and is aware of your strengths, weaknesses, abilities, and personality, is responsible for compiling this report. Depending on how long you remain with your current employer, the review could lead to a promotion and pay increases.

Let me tell you what is bad about employee performance reviews as we currently know them. They are subjective, meaning that your boss, the person who knows your work product best and is aware of your strengths, weaknesses, abilities, and personality, is responsible for compiling this report. Depending on how long you remain with your current employer, this review could lead to missed opportunities, stagnation in pay, and a lack of promotions simply because your supervisor is lazy when it comes to appraisals or just may not like you all that much.

Catch my drift? As long as companies use subjective performance reviews as a basis for promotion, pay, and bonus—but especially for promotion—they can be manipulated simply by favoritism. Does this happen? Of course it does.

THE SUBJECTIVE COMPONENT OF THE REVIEW

My stance will be obvious here, but I believe performance reviews, with proper engagement from the employee, should be weighted heavily toward the QTNT value calculation process while including only certain subjective factors. The subjective aspect of performance reviews, as we know them, can't be completely discarded. There will always be a need to measure, at a minimum, a worker's soft skills (you know: plays well with others, etc.), and there must be a place for purely subjective notes, such as "Recommend for promotion" or "Suggest additional training." There will always be a need to mention someone's leadership skills and his or her chance of successfully accepting more responsibility.

The Quotient, however, provides the employee and the employer a metric, an objective measurement: a counterbalance to the management appraisal process that has never, before now, existed for the individual worker.

Q-STUDY NO. 13

Brad: Property Management
"The Cover Sheet"

Note: The following story was recalled as I was working with a client. The event described here occurred ten years prior to our discussion, which is why actual budgeted values are not used in the calculations. This Q-Study offers a reasonable and creative look at seeking a value workaround.

Brad was the manager of an office complex—one of twenty-six his company owned across the United States. Brad found himself in some legal trouble after renewing the lease of an existing tenant, when he missed the fine print that had been handwritten into the original agreement by his predecessor several years earlier. This addition stated that the real estate agent who had introduced the client company would be paid on all future renewals. As a result of this mistake, he was sued by the originating agent for nonpayment of the renewal commission.

Realizing he had no option, Brad recommended to his boss that they pay the commission and put the issue behind them. After delivering the commission check to the originating broker, Brad returned to his office and told his office manager they were going to review all 185 leases on file at the time. He intended to create a cover sheet for each lease that would identify any changes made to the original lease documents, no matter how minor. This effort took about a week and a half, with Brad and his secretary reviewing every page of every lease, making the necessary notes, and then placing what he called his "Lease Abstract" cover sheet on the top of each lease.

A COMPANYWIDE SOLUTION

A few months later, Brad's boss, Mike, a regional vice president, dropped by the office. At the end of each visit, it was Mike's custom to randomly grab a handful of lease files and toss them out on the conference room table to review.

When Mike opened the first folder, he noticed the new cover sheet and asked Brad about it. Brad told him he had been upset about having to turn over the commission check because of a mistake he had made that should have been avoided. He added that Mike was now looking at his solution to the problem. Mike immediately recognized the benefit the cover sheet would have across the entire company. He took the concept back to the corporate office, where it was adopted for use in all twenty-six office parks.

What's important to note here is that Brad had not realized the value to the company of what he had done. He had solved a problem that had existed companywide for many years. That problem? The cost of engaging attorneys every time a property manager made a lease-renewal mistake by failing to spot the fine print inserted into previously negotiated leases. These mistakes cost the billion-dollar company a million dollars or more each year. While Brad's focus had been to remedy a situation he had incurred at the street level, he had resolved a problem that happened in some form across the company every week.

CALCULATING THE VALUE CONTRIBUTION

Brad's solution was the creation of the lease cover sheet. The net result of this accomplishment—the value contribution to the company—can be calculated based on the following information.

Brad was responsible for the profitable management of more than 400,000 net leasable square feet. The annual quoted rate per square foot at the time was $12 per foot. If you multiply those two numbers, you come up with the gross revenue Brad was charged with achieving on an annual basis if the property was to be 100% occupied.

400,000 square feet x $12 rent per net square foot =
$4,800,000 gross annual income

As anyone in the real estate business will tell you, the real estate and legal professions are joined at the hip. In addition to the cost at the corporate offices for in-house legal, each leasing office across the country had a local firm on retainer. Based on his budget and experience, Brad determined that he spent approximately 2% of his annual gross income on legal fees. In the interest of calculating his QTNT PVC conservatively, he decided to use an even lower factor of 1% that could be saved by not having to engage legal counsel for avoidable mistakes.

$4,800,000 annual income x .01 legal expense = $48,000 in legal fees

Brad's annual pay at the time was $56,000 per year. He is now able to calculate the approximate savings realized by the company when this number is multiplied by the twenty-six office parks spread across the country.

$48,000 annual legal fees saved x 26 office parks = $1,248,000

$$\frac{\text{Total approximate annual savings on legal expense } = \$1,248,000}{\text{Brad's annual pay } = \$56,000}$$

Brad's Quotient for creating his Lease Abstract cover sheet = 22.29

At 400,000 square feet, Brad managed the smallest office park in the company (some exceeded 2,000,000 net leasable square feet). By choosing to use a 1% savings factor on legal expenses, these are reasonable and highly conservative savings he can share with management at any level.

The important takeaway from this Q-Study is that you might be saving your company several hundred dollars or several thousand dollars a year, month, or week because of your efficiencies. When you begin to add up these savings across other offices, locations, or branches, you could very well be responsible for saving your company loads of money!

"Discrimination costs a lot of money and, in return, creates no value whatever."

—RICK GILLIS

31

Project Management and the Quotient

FOUNDED IN 1969, the Project Management Institute (PMI) is an organization that was founded on a brilliant concept: to teach management techniques to professionals not specifically trained in management. People who are schooled in IT or engineering or finance, for example, are taught—and, as PMI® members, are certified and continue to learn—management techniques at an accelerated pace. And it works. I know. I spoke and trained project managers in job search and personal promotion at PMI conferences and chapter meetings for over ten years. As a result, I became friends with many professional project managers and, in fact, interviewed several for this book.

To be clear, I am not a project manager. I am not a member of PMI, and I have not earned a Project Management Professional (PMP®)[4] designation. Nevertheless, I feel comfortable broadly discussing project management from an outsider's perspective.

Certified project management represents a far-reaching, "new" (since 1969!) kind of employment hierarchy that is becoming more and more accepted across the globe. Professional project management, in my view, will become the way—if not the reason—organizations will be structured in the future. In terms of employee count, corporations will decrease in size, while project managers will proliferate and become indispensable to the core mission of the organization. In defense of that statement, you might want to revisit chapter 21, "The Quotient and the Future of Employment," where I talked about the dynamics of employment following World War II and the impact retirement costs are having on the American employer.

It is because of this model that I believe project management and the

---

4   "PMI" and "PMP" are registered marks of Project Management Institute, Inc.

Quotient were made for each other. Together, these two ideas will be an integral part of the future of employment.

Enterprise will do what it must in order to survive. As previously discussed, businesses of all sizes have been placing more work in the hands of contractors whenever possible; the intent being to hire fewer permanent workers.

PROJECTS END

Projects, by design, have a beginning, a middle, and an end. If, when a job is completed, the organization does not have another project that requires the skill set of that particular PM, that person is released, saving the company a payroll expense. And, important to this discussion, the company is not on the hook for any future benefits either.

As this approach has become more prevalent, the preferred go-to contract employee has become the qualified project manager who, because of PMI's certifications, is a known entity. (Yes, I know there are project managers on corporate payrolls, but I anticipate this, too, will change over time as PMs retire or move on.)

Professional project managers who have earned the PMP designation are expected to be capable of producing high-level, specialized work in their field of expertise while also having the ability to oversee and successfully manage the workforce dynamics of a project. This is because the controls and leadership components of the PMP are conceptually well aligned with what a person would learn in a traditional university business program.

The PMP designation, then, confirms for the employer that this employee is not only skilled and educated in his or her primary skill set but also able to manage a team, a budget, and a project, thus filling the shoes of several workers for the price of one. The PMP certification is somewhat comparable to an undergrad degree in management or even, as one moves up the PMI learning ladder, an MBA.

PROJECT MANAGERS AND THE QUOTIENT

Now you can see how the Quotient comes into focus for PMs. When a project manager is available and competing for a new assignment within his or her current company—or going on the bench and competing with other similarly qualified PMs—an understanding and application of the

QTNT PVC process can tilt the playing field to that person's advantage. An outstanding Quotient score, indicating superior performance on previous projects, can make all the difference among PMs seeking the same position.

32 Independent Contractors, PMs, and the Quotient

U NLIKE TRADITIONAL EMPLOYEES, contractors and independent project managers must know all of their costs going in. This is accomplished by determining their fully burdened labor rate, which will include personal pay, mandatory taxes, Social Security, and the cost of travel, time, tools, software, equipment, and any other outlays that may be a required expense of the contractor, such as insurance and permits that can be justifiably allocated to the job.

If you are an electrician—a contractor—and you come to my office to do some work, I can expect that you will have on hand the supplies and tools as well as the necessary licenses, insurance, and permits to get the job done at the quoted rate. Because of your expertise in the field, you can usually give me a pretty fair idea of what the job will cost even before we agree you should make the trip. That agreed-on price may be subject to modification when you arrive on-site and see that the problem is not as I had initially described it.

This same scenario applies to an independent project manager or contractor who accepts a project. As a contractor, you are, at least at the outset, operating in a "perfect world." You (or the agent representing you) have bid on the job, so you know your return (wages) going in. A cost-benefit analysis has been performed by the project owner, and assuming the proposal is successfully executed, a perfect Quotient of 1 can effectively be predetermined. Right? Not likely. All kinds of things happen on projects. And, of course, a project manager is seeking not just to get the job done while delivering top-flight results but also to achieve a positive-plus Quotient score.

YOUR PROJECT-MANAGING QUOTIENT

Although it is up to you to determine your Quotient, as a contractor, its value may be defined and "at the mercy" of the employer, client, or project owner. Because of this, you need to be able to break down the variables that make up your PVC and be prepared to present those values. Once again, I implore you to always err on the conservative side. Never present sky-high returns on previous projects unless you have the supporting documentation or references to back them up. This is a crucial aspect of the work of a project manager and the reason I say that the Quotient methodology and process is a natural tool for the professional project manager to embrace.

Review the Q-Studies throughout this book. Several of them are stories of actual project managers I advised. Each of these studies provides sufficient detail or, at minimum, enough guidance for you to be able to walk your way through your own past projects. Why? Because the Quotient process and your ability to know it forward and backward prepares you for the interview. When you next apply for a project management position, you want to be able to not only present what you did previously but also provide your potential employer with a QTNT PVC rating for that performance. For example, you can show him or her how you were able to exceed a QTNT score of 16 on your last three projects combined. If they are not familiar with the Quotient, you can share how you delivered value sixteen times what you were paid.

One more point. Organizations often hire contract PMs to "audition" them with the intent of making a full-time offer if they make the grade. Besides all the other ideas presented in this chapter, this consideration alone is reason enough for all working project managers to know how to calculate their Quotient.

Q-STUDY NO. 14

Hannah: Software Implementation Manager

"Shorting Her Pay"

Hannah provided me with a list of accomplishments. This one jumped out at me because I can see, as will you, a few different ways her score could be calculated.

At the time, Hannah was a software implementation manager for a food brokerage firm with more than eighty separate entities operating under the corporate umbrella. The company was in need of a complete overhaul of warehouse workflow processes and an inventory control system responsible for tracking thousands of products. A major focus was on the product-scanning translation software that had to be, as you can imagine, spectacularly flawless with so many items requiring unique identification.

Hannah was tasked with implementing the software platform her supervisors purchased "off the shelf." This meant Hannah and her team were assigned the responsibility for making all modifications necessary for this program to be fully functional within the parameters required of the brokerage.

After an initial six-month trial, Hannah was given the responsibility of managing the planned five-year project budgeted at $10,500,000. Her big win came when she was able to successfully get the job completed two years early, saving the company loads of money.

To complete this calculation, you need to know that Hannah's rate of pay was $80,000 per year. The implementation budget, as you already know, was $10,500,000, or $2,100,000 per year for the five years originally projected.

QTNT CALCULATION #1:

For establishing a basis only, *had* Hannah brought the original $10,500,000 implementation on line in five years according to plan, her QTNT score would have been

$$\frac{\$10,500,000 \text{ (total five-year implementation budget)}}{\$400,000 \text{ (Hannah's projected five-year salary)}} = 26.25$$

Her PVC for a perfect performance, based on the initial budget, would have been 26.25.

QTNT CALCULATION #2:

But since she brought the project to completion and shaved two years' worth of costs off the project, Hannah's Quotient should be calculated as follows (remember that a QTNT score can be based on revenue *or* savings):

$$\frac{2 \text{ years of saved/unspent funds } = \$4,200,000}{\text{Hannah's salary x the 3 years she was paid } = \$240,000}$$

QTNT Score = 17.5

This method of viewing Hannah's achievement looks at total savings derived by completing the installation two years early, divided by the total pay Hannah received during her three years of work. From this perspective, her QTNT score equals 17.5 and is 8.75 points less than calculation #1.

QTNT CALCULATION # 3:

Another way Hannah could view this calculation would be by taking the savings for the final two years and dividing that total by her salary for the year (only) in which this savings took place, which was her final (or third year) on the project:

$$\frac{\$4,200,000 \text{ (2 years of unspent budget saved)}}{\$80,000 \text{ (a single year's salary)}} = 52.5$$

As you can see, because there are several different "moving parts" in this accomplishment, Hannah can theoretically present this PVC from the point of view that best supports *her* interests—which would be the third version, which is, honestly, in kind of a gray area. In her exit interview the most important consideration would be the strength of her defensible statements.

I leave it up to you to decide which presentation would be the most "correct," but in my humble opinion, I think all three have merit—as long as she can explain them.

Regardless of which way you view her accomplishment, Hannah delivered outstanding value for her work. On the job, her employer would determine which calculation to use, while she alone would decide how she might share this accomplishment with any future employers.

Finally, Hannah's Accomplishments Statement should read something like this:

> *Responsible for bringing a planned five-year, $10,500,000 software configuration and implementation project to a successful conclusion two years ahead of schedule, saving the enterprise $4,200,000.*

Also worth noting is that, by coming in ahead of schedule, she personally "shorted" herself two years' worth of salary, or $160,000, while saving the company money. How many people might have chosen to sandbag the project and stretch it out two more years?

33 Open-Book Management

OPEN-BOOK MANAGEMENT is a relatively little-known but nimble people-management style that works exceptionally well in tandem with the Quotient. Open-book management is what the name implies: its success depends on management's willingness to "open the books" to their employees regardless of the size of the company.

OBM was invented in 1983 through sheer necessity by Jack Stack, as described in his book *The Great Game of Business*. Stack and his co-investors made a potentially ruinous revenue assumption when acquiring their first company and very quickly realized that all hands—with an emphasis on "all"—were needed on deck if the new company had any chance of surviving. What Stack decided was that all those hands needed to be educated to understand just how dire things were. It was then that he began teaching and sharing the company's financial reports—the books—with his workers. Now you know why it's called open-book management.

Interviewing OBM experts John Case and Bill Fotsch, I learned that the engaged business owner will initially provide only that financial information *relevant* to each employee's job—that is, what they do for the organization. Educating workers in the meaning of those reports in brief, weekly sessions teaches them how, for example, just 10% more effort or production on their part could significantly benefit the company as well as themselves.

You may have heard that employers want to hire only those people who "think like an owner." The OBM methodology trains workers to think like an owner, and the Quotient, by extension, measures that delivery.

SHARING THE WINS

There is another critical aspect to OBM that virtually ensures it will work. When your employees think like owners and their output increases accordingly—regardless of what they do for you—they share in the win. In other words, if Pablo gets so good at his job that he is now producing fifteen warranty-worthy, functioning widgets a month compared to his previous best of eight a month, he is entitled to share in the benefits the company realizes for his efforts. It's bonus time! Regular bonuses reinforce the program, and workers truly do come to "own" their jobs. They actually do think and act in the best interests of the company.

To traditionally trained and educated managers, OBM may sound a bit idyllic, but it's not. OBM is in place in numerous small businesses across the country and even in divisions of some of the most famous companies whose names you would recognize.

CONFIDENTIALITY

So, you might ask, what about confidentiality? Isn't my expert, skilled tradesman, Pablo, going to share company secrets with his buddies after work at the neighborhood watering hole? Well, maybe and maybe not, but what does it matter?

All businesses have the same costs. Think about that. All businesses pay for labor, rent, inventory, raw materials, taxes, et cetera at relatively the same rate. None of this is "confidential," because the competition already knows this information. More importantly, management only shares that information workers need to know. Maybe more to the point is the idea that Pablo, thinking like an owner now, will be more inclined to protect "his"—and "their"—common interests.

One last thought on OBM: Useful information travels in both directions. When Pablo knows how to read the financials, the conversation becomes two-way. When he can offer up new products or big cost savings by finding a better way of doing something, management will know they have an "owner" on the team.

34 The Overhead Expense Discussion

IF YOU ARE a manager, an owner, a CFO, or a CEO, I am certain you are acutely aware that I kept the cost of overhead for employees *out* of the QTNT Personal Value Calculation up until now. This was by design.

Since the Quotient is a new and robust concept, I decided at the outset not to saddle my audience with the inclusion and calculation of overhead costs until the QTNT PVC process was fully explained. Frankly, unless it's their job to do so, most employees don't give a thought to how much it costs the company to open the doors and turn on the lights, even as everything the company pays for surrounds them.

When your company is ready to implement the Quotient, a fairly simple solution to this problem would be for each operating unit to establish a single, separate factor—a burden—to account for all those "other expenses" as a percentage of each employee's all-in cost to the business. This factor is already known by accounting and can be handled with a keystroke or two in your accounting or human resources information system (HRIS).

Another way to deal with these overhead costs may be to handle them in the open-book management style discussed in chapter 33. In the OBM model, the organization shares *relevant* expenses with employees. OBM also promotes the sharing of any windfall this process creates for the company in the form of bonuses back to the workers. The result is that the company has a motivated and more knowledgeable workforce watching out for the company's cost of doing business and, by extension, profits. They, your employees, can then calculate their own expense costs, which is a terrific way to validate their cost/expense awareness and further enhance their on-the-floor engagement.

Regardless of what method your organization might apply to incorporate overhead costs, they are included in the weighting of each position that I will share with you in chapter 37, "Position-Based Weighting and the Quotient."

35 Engagement: Thinking Like an Owner

YOU MAY KNOW about the Hawthorne effect, a term used to describe a short-lived increase in employee productivity, which came out of a series of studies conducted in the 1920s and '30s. The goal was to determine how to best engage a specific team of workers. Lighting, both bright and dim, was tried, as was the modification of working hours, changes to the immediate environment, and more. In the end, the research concluded that employees became more engaged as a *result of being observed*—it was the attention, not the environment, that made the most difference. Although other conclusions came from the Hawthorne studies, this observation has stuck with me since my Management 101 days. These workers, performing monotonous but important assembly work, were, to put it simply, craving attention, which being studied generated. Attention and appreciation, in my opinion, happen to be the means to achieving employee engagement. Good pay doesn't hurt either!

Engagement, or as I have called it throughout the book, "thinking like an owner," is simply employee commitment, and the result, by extension, is retention. I don't have to tell any manager that people are expensive. New people, even more so. Observation and management's active participation is, obviously, a large component of engagement.

The Quotient provides its own "Hawthorne effect" by providing hands-on training and observation. Employees, individually, learn to watch for their above-and-beyond-the-job-description efforts that they can share with management. The Quotient turbocharges the right kind of active management participation to further perfect this engagement.

I'm no psychologist, but simply put: when your employees are actively involved in their own careers to a level where they can give their all and realize a benefit, they actually will begin thinking like an owner.

Pie in the sky? Well, yes—and no. Studies currently suggest that employee engagement hovers somewhere between 15% and 40% (ouch!). We can agree that no company will ever be able to get all employees to engage at the commitment level management longs for, but if an organization can get X% more employees thinking this way, can that be bad? Will that percentage grow as workers benefit from and become evangelists for the Quotient? I think as the word gets around, then, to some degree, yes.

TANGIBLE BENEFITS

"Thinking like an owner" means getting your employees into the accomplishments mindset. Once your employees realize they can be in charge of their own destiny, and they see that bonuses, promotions, and raises (and new houses, and new cars, and cool vacations, etc.) are the results of this effort, they will be motivated to achieve higher and better Quotient scores, which, in turn, benefits the organization.

36 The Quotient and Proper Pay

I N MY OPINION, the pay parity discussion is not as much about equal pay for equal work as it is about *the right pay—the proper pay—for the value delivered to the organization, regardless of who delivers it.* I know employers will agree with this. There will always be a salary floor, a base rate for each position in the company, that will be dictated by the market. The Quotient does not change the requirement for a company to be competitive on the street, but it does offer a "newish" form of compensation for non-sales workers. Newish because companies already know how to compensate commissioned professionals.

With the Quotient in place, your staff, all of them, can begin thinking (don't misquote me here) *somewhat* like a commissioned sales employee who is required to meet a standard (=1) before earning a bonus. Those employees who actively embrace the Quotient will become the "half" who do all the work for our CEO, the one I mentioned in the first sentence of chapter 1.

Once employees are on board, have been coached on the benefits of the Quotient, and learn how they can, to some degree, control their rate of pay and by extension their career, they will begin thinking like owners. They will begin seeking ways to contribute additional value to the company, knowing there is more than a one-time bonus in store for their efforts.

All of this will take commitment to the Quotient on the part of the organization. The way to ramp up this effort will be a test run with a single department, section, or branch. Instruction in all aspects of the Quotient is the key.

AVOIDING A STAMPEDE

As you know, women currently make about 80 cents for each dollar a man is paid for the same work. I believe employers are a bit off balance trying to figure out how to get equalizing pay to those wronged parties (my term, not theirs). The goal, of course, is to (1) prevent a stampede of talent for those who will not receive this pay increase (note I did not say "raise") while (2) providing increases to only those on the payroll who verifiably deserve them. Let's face it: not everyone who thinks they are doing equal work—as defined by a company's "equal pay for equal work" criteria—is.

This is not just about gender. This consideration takes into account those affected by race, disability, sex, age, ethnicity, and more. This can be resolved with the Quotient because an employer, with an employee's active participation, can now measure a worker's return on their investment in a way that has never been able to be done before.

SPEAKING TO JUST MEN FOR A MINUTE . . .

Guys, women are graduating from college at higher rates than men and have been for some time. In five to ten years, if not sooner, management will "more equally" be comprised of both sexes and all kinds of populations. No longer will a woman who has been promoted to CEO of a Fortune 100 company be news. Gen Z is growing up more inclusive than previous generations, as will the generations that follow. This is as it should be.

Since women make as much as 80% of consumer buying decisions, paying women properly is *very* good for the economy—any economy! Besides, discrimination costs a *lot* of money and, in return, creates no value whatever. In any event, every person—and this includes men—*will* be age-discriminated against at some point in his or her working life. Count on it. Steel thyself!

SOME MORE HISTORY

The US, seventy-five years on, is still dealing with a post–World War II hangover whereby the myth persists that a woman "doesn't need" to be paid as well as a man because "she is being supported by a husband." News flash, folks: we don't listen to fireside chats anymore, and our phones are no longer attached to a wall. (For my younger readers who do not know what I'm talking about, Google it.)

There are no good reasons as to why this unequal pay trend continues. Because "it's always been that way" is a tragically lame excuse.

THE QUOTIENT AND PAY BASED ON PERFORMANCE

As the QTNT formula, **C** ÷ **P** (Verified Value of Employee's **Contribution** ÷ Employee's Base **Pay**), moves into the mainstream, as more and more companies and workers learn what the QTNT PVC process is and how to determine the value of their contribution, equal or *greater* pay will result for the person who earns it. As a company receives measurably exceptional value from an employee, the company creates a self-fulfilling prophecy by paying that person well. Winners will rise to the top regardless of what they look like, what they believe in, or how old they are.

When employees have more control over their authentic and perceived value, when they begin thinking "like an employer" and can present and defend their value to the company in a meaningful manner, a lot of the struggles that employers currently deal with daily will simply vanish. Once again I ask, pie in the sky? Maybe yes. Maybe not.

In chapter 19, "Equal Pay or the Proper Pay?" I wrote: "More pay, appropriate promotion, and bonuses for better work are the goals all individuals strive for. Conversely and appropriately, more production and bigger returns are the corporation's goals." We are, after all, in this together. The Quotient, with the proper implementation, education, and oversight, can make proper pay a reality.

37 Position-Based Weighting and the Quotient

SIMILAR TO MY deliberately turning a blind eye to the issue of corporate overhead expense up to this point, I also avoided the issue of assigning a weighted value to each position in the organization—until now. Again, I reasoned it was important for the individual reader to focus on the value of his or her work by witnessing those remarkable numbers posted by real people in the Q-Studies, rather than to throw weighting into the discussion and create unnecessary confusion.

> SIDENOTE: An organization may well choose to disregard this idea of weighting altogether and treat measured accomplishment as I have done in the Q-Studies.

Notwithstanding any laws, employment agreements, or safety issues that would not allow for the establishment of weighted performance minimums, QTNT scores based on the Contribution ÷ Pay formula, especially at the time of hire, can be thought of as a performance agreement between employees and employers. Weighting can be viewed as employer-established benchmarks (not to be confused with KPIs) that workers must meet in order to be considered reasonably successful in their jobs.

By establishing an attainable or targeted weighted metric, employers are signaling that employees are expected to perform at a level equal to, and preferably well above, their pay grade. To successfully participate, new employees will need to be educated in all aspects of the Quotient process during the onboarding process. They will learn how their performance will be measured as well as how to measure the same on their own, especially any above-and-beyond-the-call-of-duty achievements.

They will learn the accomplishments mindset. (If you think about it, there is actually not much difference here between a salesperson's employment agreement and the requisite product sales training.)

WHAT WEIGHTING LOOKS LIKE

The goal of weighting is to create a company of =1s across the board. These =1s would be the minimum delivery of work product expected of each employee, the result being a "well-oiled machine." Weighting is based on performance exclusively. Although performance contribution is a sibling to pay, bonuses, options, et cetera, money has nothing to do with weighting. This is only about performance.

So, what does weighting look like? Well, for example, a $300,000-a-year rock-star coder who is weighted 10x would achieve an =1 rating upon delivering a $3,000,000 performance value in a fiscal year. (The period for the completion of a weighted project can be variable and stated in months, quarters, or even multiple years.)

Real wins happen when a weighted worker's =1 is exceeded. The rank or skill set of the person makes no difference. An =1+ (>1) is a win at any position at any time. (For a refresher, you might want to review chapter 3, "Three Kinds of QTNT Scores.")

In an ideal business world, no employees in an organization would ever score less than their position's weighted =1. Business nirvana? Sure. But because of the Quotient, this is a measurable—and adjustable—goal the organization can strive for when the employee is an active participant in the outcome.

Quotient weighting, then, can be used to establish a floor in terms of expected delivery of value by all employees, line or staff, at every pay grade. The larger the weight, the more important the position is to the success of the company. Weighting requires annual review to determine that a weight remains accurate based on the market as well as performance. Weighting must be flexible enough to allow for economic upticks or downturns. Weighting may also need to be adjusted or even suspended for unproven new talent coming on board. In short, weighting must be both dynamic and flexible.

38 Quotient Weighting in Practice

A FORKLIFT DRIVER IS earning his =1 at $35,000 a year. But what about our prodigy coder, mentioned in the previous chapter, who is brought on to lead the creation of the next big thing at $300,000 annual base plus? Should he or she be weighted ten times ($3,000,000 equals an =1) or twenty times ($6,000,000 equals an =1) or a hundred times ($30,000,000 equals an =1) annual pay in order to be considered successful? The nature of the need and the employee's résumé, history in the space, interview, and assessment will play into this determination. With both parties agreeing to accept the responsibilities of such a large weight, this agreement may require adjustment or fine-tuning after an initial period of engagement. The market, budgets, and the company's willingness to gamble on this candidate all play into a weighting calculation. Such would not be the case with our forklift operator.

I know what I'm suggesting here is a "slice" of a brave new world of sorts. There is no hard science for me to refer to, but I think you can see how this could become performance measurement science in compensation circles.

Our coder is a one-off—but not unrealistic—example of weighting that requires individual attention. He or she could just as well be an engineer or a pharmaceutical chemist of unparalleled talent. For most positions in an organization, this would not be the case. Except for seismic earners, the head of compensation in concert with management would assign a weight for each position in the company. The board of directors may just as easily determine a weighted Quotient for the CEO and other C-suite tenants.

POSITION VS. PERSON

Again, do not confuse the term *position* with a living, breathing person. Personalities do not enter into the calculation. This is about the job as it is required to be performed for the benefit and success of the company—the training, experience, and qualifications required of someone to occupy that seat, not the person who is holding the position. Once the individual is in place, weighting can be adjusted for fit.

Your company will determine a flexible but "ideal" weighting factor for each position, allowing for variances while remaining within range. Once engaged in this process, HR, accounting, and management will likely acquire new and useful information never before realized.

Over time industries will determine "ideal" QTNT weights for virtually all positions within their scope of interest. Someone, somewhere, perhaps in academia if not in private practice, will study and create a Quotient-based weighting index or an algorithm that will include all potential variables to assign an "ideal weight" for each job title as listed by the US Bureau of Labor Statistics (BLS.gov).

Lastly, compensation levels, in line with market conditions and demand, can be more accurately established based on the return of an employer's investment in an individual. The more both parties in a hiring conversation know about what is expected at the outset of an employment arrangement (e.g., "We anticipate a return on your hire on the order of 3.7 times your annual salary, expenses, and benefits."), the less angst there will be in the employee-employer relationship.

39 The Baseline Audit

O NE DEFINITION OF *baseline* is "a starting point that can be used for comparisons," which is a perfect place to begin this discussion on why a company may want to consider initiating a baseline audit of all employees upon implementation of the Quotient.

THE QUOTIENT BASELINE

Human resources will obviously be tasked with the implementation of the Quotient, but all department heads, a dedicated enterprise resource planning (ERP) IT pro, and, of course, your compensation specialist, at a minimum, will be actively involved.

I don't see this as an absolute requirement for the introduction of the Quotient, or even for its long-term use, but it might be helpful for the organization to know each employee's approximate Quotient at the outset and determine an appropriate performance value that should be expected assuming it is not already known. Conducting such a baseline for staff might reveal some surprising gems among the ranks you may not currently be aware of.

Each employee's current performance can be baselined and compared with individuals performing the same kind of work using the Quotient model. This is not meant to be a house cleaning—on the contrary. This effort will provide each worker and management a mutual starting point to learn the Quotient. Everyone will share in the learning curve.

To restate, the QTNT PVC is the result of the employee's Value of Contribution divided by their Base Pay.

This is also the ideal time to identify those workers whose work qualifies them for a Quotient of 1 (=1), less than 1 (<1), or the Exempt designation, which may excuse them from being scored altogether. (See chapter 4, "Three Ways of Looking at a Q < 1," for more on the exempt status.)

An =1 designation, as you know, is most often identified with those workers who return a value (more or less) equal to what they earn. An example of this might be a dependable and reliable warehouse worker or delivery person.

Boards of directors might want to have a say in senior management Quotient contribution measurement. A CEO's numbers are usually public, and as such, that person's Quotient would be reasonably easy to calculate. Other C-level personnel values might not be as simple to quantify, which makes them a qualified target for measurement.

EDUCATING STAFF ON THE QUOTIENT

All employees require education on the mechanics and the rationale behind the Quotient and how it will benefit them personally, especially when they learn they are, more than ever before, in charge of their future with the company.

For those employees engaged in the sales process, the concept of determining their value to the company is a foregone conclusion. Your sales team, as well as management and department heads, already live and die based on "the daily numbers." Nevertheless, all sales professionals should be included in the initial house audit and the education process.

As I have said several times throughout the book, I'm not as concerned about the sales team. Sales departments exist in their own ecosystem. It's everyone else that I'm concerned about. Again, most employees don't sell, but rather, support the sale or delivery of a product or service. From the folks in research to those who support the warranty, they are, to a large degree, those people who do their jobs, do them well, and assume there will be more orders, more accounting, and more deliveries to be made tomorrow. These people may have varying levels of understanding of how their work directly impacts the bottom line. (There are always exceptions, of course, but you get my drift.)

The Quotient will identify those employees who consider their job as merely a means to a paycheck as well as the hard-charging, profit-generating SVP determined to exceed last year's numbers by 30%. Every company requires =1s, but no company can survive, much less excel, without those +10s, +30s, and more.

NON-REVENUE-GENERATING EMPLOYEES

My professional employment mantra has always been *you either make money for a company or you save money for a company.* If you can't do one or the other, you will not keep your job.

I recognize that this idea of determining how much value a non-revenue-generating employee contributes to their company is foreign to most, if not all, of your hourly and even some salaried workers. In my coaching practice I have watched as many professionals found it difficult to grasp the concept that they make money for the organization by being efficient, by *saving* money, by doing their job better than anyone else, and by striving for the highest and best outcome for the enterprise. In short, by knowing and understanding their commercial value. I can honestly say that, of the hundreds and hundreds of people I have counseled in job search and advancement, only a handful were in sales. This is because salespeople inherently understand job search—which is selling.

Most workers don't think in terms of sales or revenue—until things go south, and then it is usually too late for them to consider their contribution to the whole, if they even do so then.

Let me provide you with an example of how a non-revenue-generating employee can deliver remarkable value to an organization while not having that value specifically noted in the dollars-in column.

An in-house attorney is not on staff to create revenue but rather to position and defend the organization when necessary. When this attorney successfully defends her client, her company, from a $100,000 unlawful termination claim that is reduced to a zero payout, she can claim a verifiably defensible savings for the company of $100,000. Even though no entry will be made in the books for the "hard" savings accrued, she can keep a ledger of such savings (wins) and justifiably present them in her QTNT calculations and for performance review consideration.

This example points out the necessity of educating your workforce on the Quotient and teaching them to think like owners, regardless of age or position.

40 Why Industry Detests Performance Appraisals

AH, PERFORMANCE APPRAISALS! Performance appraisals have been getting a bad rap for decades. Search for yourself and see how much negative stuff has been written by highly prominent organizations (whose names you would know) about why they don't work.

As management guru W. Edwards Deming said so wisely decades ago, *"The most basic problem is that performance appraisals often don't accurately assess performance."* So, besides the anxiety they cause, they don't appraise performance either.

More recently, Cy Wakeman of Reality-Based Leadership said, *"Unfortunately, the most common and usually only feedback an employee gets from their managers tells them very little about where they actually stand and how much value they are contributing to the bottom line."*

So, with that cheery open, I plan on spending the next few pages telling you why current performance appraisals don't work. But I won't wreak havoc without offering a nifty solution, one that makes common sense, is simple to implement, and works. (By the way, KPIs? They are never going away. How well they are or are not written is a topic for another book.)

WHY CURRENT PERFORMANCE APPRAISALS FAIL

- *Performance appraisals are subjective.*

    Subjective appraisals allow for a manager to potentially thumbs-up or thumbs-down an employee based on little more than personality (or gender or race or age . . .).

    Subjectivity resides on the surface. I have no doubt there is someone in your business unit about whom everyone wonders how the heck "they got there." If they aren't related to the boss, well, now you know. The bottom line is that some people end up in management the old-fashioned way—a buddy wrote a less-than-honest review.

- *Appraisals take anywhere from 10% to 40% of a manager's time annually.*

    When I first learned this, I found it pretty hard to believe (40%! Really?). So, of course, I did what anyone else would do to verify a fact: I went online, and yep, there it was. The "standard" metric appears to be about 10% to 20%, but some highly regarded HR sources do claim that up to 40% of a manager's time annually is spent on employee appraisal. When you put dollars to these figures, it is truly an unbelievable waste of resources and a serious loss of productivity that can never be recovered.

    Let's see: 2,080 hours (40 hours per week x 52 weeks) x 40% = 832 hours, or more than *twenty weeks* of lost production from a manager responsible for conducting and submitting who knows how many personnel appraisals.

    Utilizing a factor of 10%, which I think is a conservative number for hours a company is paying to not receive any return, the result is "only" 208 hours, which is still more than five forty-hour weeks a year of lost production. Multiply that by a single manager's pay, and then multiply that by the number of managers in your organization, and voila! A few thousand dollars here and several thousand dollars there, and pretty soon you are throwing away some real money!

- *Individual employees are estimated to spend approximately forty hours preparing for their appraisal.*

    Because current appraisals will have such a large impact on their future as well as the percentage of their participation in the bonus pool, employees put a good amount of time into preparing for them. Now, you don't think they are doing this week's worth of prep on their own time, do you? How many employees do you have again?

- *The "glowing" performance appraisal costs your organization even more when presented as evidence.*

    On occasion, your company may have to defend against a wrongful termination case. At almost every one of these hearings, your lawyers will have two or three or more of your former worker's employee-of-the-year-caliber performance appraisals tossed in their face by opposing counsel. Why? Let's look at a few possible reasons:

- Your manager was intimidated by the process and sold out, providing an unearned "glowing" review. (How many other similarly biased reviews are out there?)
- Your manager simply did not know enough or was just lazy and wanted to get the required appraisals over and done with.
- Your manager might have been concerned with reprisal.
- Your manager may have been one of those who provides unwarranted ratings to friends.

I'm sure everyone who works can come up with even more reasons why appraisals are a drain on the company, expensive, and not necessarily all that useful. Now let's talk about a solution.

41 Big 5 Performance Management

I T IS SOMEWHAT universally accepted that existing performance management platforms are the best of a bad system. They are expensive, and, as I have pointed out, there is the loss of value and value creation by employees at all levels who are conducting and/or preparing for them instead of doing their revenue-generating, money-saving jobs. For some companies, this loss runs into millions of dollars.

Currently performance management assessments operate more or less in this manner:

- Goal setting is done by each employee at the beginning of the year. KPIs are established.

- A review and a possible realignment of goals happen at a midyear review. Maybe.

- A year-end report is prepared by the employee.

- The final, formal review between employee and manager is conducted, signed by both parties, and posted to the employee's personnel file.

After interviewing several HR pros for this book, the consensus appears to be that the only use for this kind of appraisal is to arrive at a score that determines an employee's bonus and to get any "issues" on the record. There is a lot of noise made about employee alignment and promotions, but I wasn't hearing that.

A BETTER WAY

Might there be a better system? One that begins with a conversation well before appraisal time between an employee and his or her manager?

There is, and it's based on a monthly ten-minute, one-on-one employee-manager meeting as developed by former JPMorgan Chase Bank senior vice president of human resources Roger Ferguson, author of *Finally! Performance Assessment that Works: Big 5 Performance Management.* Big 5 offers a fresh perspective on managing and appraising employees in an ongoing, two-way conversation. The results and the savings, both in time and treasure, are remarkable.

In the course of about 120 minutes a year, a manager using the Big 5 system has face time with each employee and will more accurately know what every individual is doing and has accomplished by year-end. The Big 5 appraisal is jointly documented by both the employee and their manager one step at a time over the course of twelve months. At the end of the year, each appraisal is effectively, "informally" complete. I say "informally" because Big 5 is a continuous, ongoing process that does not specifically call for an end-of-year review. However, since virtually all companies require an end-of-year report for promotion, a bonus, and pay raises, and for the employee's permanent file, the traditional nine-box grid[5] tool works perfectly well to fulfill this requirement.

But wait a minute! What about the Quotient? What is all this Big 5 stuff about? The answer is simple. The alignment between Big 5 and the Quotient is seamless. I'll let Roger tell you a little bit more about Big 5, and then I'll point out how these two systems dovetail to the benefit of management, save money and time, and produce appreciable, real-world results.

WHAT IS BIG 5 PERFORMANCE MANAGEMENT?

As Ferguson says:

> *Big 5 promotes performance assessment that, like sales, is quick and meaningful, focuses the employee's efforts on the highest priorities, and creates accountability for better overall management of the company.*
>
> *Big 5 is a simple process that asks each employee to identify his or her five most significant accomplishments from the last reporting period and five highest priorities for the next reporting period.*

Big 5 performance management is different because it asks employees to own the process of documenting their plans and contributions

---

5   See glossary for a description of the nine-box grid.

(engagement, anyone?) by answering two straightforward questions:

1. What are the five most significant achievements the employee has made in the last reporting period (the past month)?
2. What are the five highest priorities for the next reporting period?

HOW BIG 5 AND THE QUOTIENT WORK WELL TOGETHER

When it comes to the Quotient, the QTNT valuation process, and Big 5 working in tandem, it will become evident to you that Big 5 does the "heavy lifting" by creating an accomplishments inventory that is expanded monthly. In the first half of the book I explained the process of sourcing and identifying an employee's best personal wins and calculating a value for each. Big 5 accomplishes this thought-provoking process on a monthly basis.

Employees get into the habit of thinking about identifying personal wins and making note of them. While I recommend that each employee maintain a daily calendar/diary of performance reminders, Big 5 *compels* this effort to the employer's–and the employee's–benefit. You want employee engagement? You want your employees to think like owners? Big 5 and the Quotient make this happen!

Big 5 is flexible. It allows for the individual employee to address "other accomplishments," not necessarily just the monthly five. Getting your employees, regardless of position or rank, thinking in terms of defining their successes and determining the value of their contributions to the company every month, rather than just once or twice a year, is a big win for the company.

Ferguson also wisely points out one of the more significant flaws of traditional appraisal systems:

> *Tying individual goals to corporate goals is difficult if not impossible. Most corporate goals are not defined specifically enough to translate well to individual performance.*

For example, can someone working in a battery fabrication plant for an electric car company genuinely relate to the corporate mandate that three new models will be on the road by year-end?

Ferguson goes on to say:

> *Employees know the drill and, for the most part, practice patience and conformity in completing the process. But the bottom line with [the traditional] type of program is that just about everyone involved*

sees the process as a compliance exercise only. The reason they partici-pate is because Human Resources requires it.

Does this make the Quotient and Big 5 disruptors in the perfor-mance review space? Yes.

42 The Big 5-Q Performance Model

THE QUOTIENT AND Big 5 together are tools that can positively change the performance appraisal business as it currently exists with little disruption.

As you saw in the previous chapter, Big 5 does the incremental "heavy lifting" of producing a monthly accomplishments inventory with a superb, documented, end-of-year wrap-up. Big 5 provides consistent attention and alignment with employee KPIs and keeps all the players, both employees and management, engaged and tuned in to any big wins as well as any issues that should be addressed—all in real time.

For those workers who actively engage in the process, the Quotient provides a mechanism to source, value, and present their regular work as well as over-and-above-the-call-of-duty accomplishments that are beneficial to the organization. Each monthly or annual QTNT score is the result of employee-manager participation.

OBJECTIVE VS. SUBJECTIVE MEASUREMENT

Let's see what things might look like if the Big 5–Quotient were utilized by industry instead of current performance appraisal systems.

The Big 5–Q performance model replaces subjective reviews with an *objective* measurement of an employee's work contribution based on actual numbers. If the company's accounting system is robust enough to track virtually all expenses (e.g., as in a hospital) and how those expenses apply to each worker, expense values could be provided to employees in real time, in-house, and tendered to employees to be defended in meetings with their managers. This model provides all employees with the opportunity to describe, value, and calculate a QTNT PVC on their own for any achievement they own.

As a result of compiling accomplishments monthly, your team will always have a good idea of where they stand. How? Your staff will be informed of their PVCs on a regularly scheduled basis or by accessing their personal online Big 5–Q profile.

43

The Quotient as a Hiring Tool

I N THE FIRST sentence of the first chapter of this book, I offered up a lame joke that I have referred back to several times: "A CEO was asked how many people work for the company, and the answer was 'About half.'"

There is a lot of truth in that statement. This is the stuff that keeps recruiters, hiring managers, and senior management up at night. As an employer, you are continuously seeking rock stars from the street, the competition, and from within.

Companies hire talent at great expense. When they do find that right person, their objective is to sell that person on the job and then retain them for a meaningful period of time. Everybody working in the hiring space faces this dilemma. The data scientists and psychologists continue to come up with new and "better" ways to hire only those who meet or exceed expectations. But let's face it: everybody is on their best behavior during the courting—er, interviewing and assessment process. Often companies don't end up with the quality of talent they thought they were getting, or they get the talent but the personality is not a fit. A good portion of payroll has been squandered, and terminating is its own expense. And so it goes.

I propose that companies may want to integrate the Quotient into their hiring process with the focus on *measurable* accomplishment as a first hurdle a candidate will encounter. This has been my practice and was my "secret sauce" in job search, where I originated the Quotient concept. In fact, the QTNT process and this book came out of my twenty-years-long practice of prepping job- and promotion-seeking professionals. In that role, I informed each potential client, up front, that they would be *required* to compile a detailed list of personal, best professional accomplishments. Doing so prepped them for a successful interview and crafting an accomplishments-based résumé. Upon completion, they would submit their résumé-quality Accomplishments Statement along with their résumé for any position they sought.

Besides having something with which to "sell" (themselves), each client was now prepped to deal with any possible value-add (think: behavioral) questions that might come up during the interview process. I told clients to expect that their résumé would be set aside during the interview as employers would be more interested in talking to them about how they could make the company money or save the company money. Over and over, I heard back that résumés were, indeed, set off to the side at the interview.

THE QUOTIENT HIRING SURVEY

Once a job applicant has been moved to candidate status and has successfully passed the initial phone interview, the candidate should be offered a Quotient-based survey and informed that the quicker this survey is completed, the quicker he or she can be scheduled for an in-person interview. This step potentially allows for a lot of valuable information to be acquired by the company prior to the interview.

What kind of information might that be? Well, the goal of the survey would be to determine if a prospective candidate has produced any currently relevant measurable achievements that would support consideration for the position being sought. The status or level of the work would make no difference as this survey would suit all applicants and discriminate against none—important for equal employment reasons.

Employers will provide the survey to the candidate with a brief primer and a couple of examples explaining how the QTNT score is determined. Candidates will be asked to identify wins, with contribution values, if possible, from previous positions and do their best to determine a QTNT score based on their then rate of pay for each. If a candidate is unable to determine a score, at minimum the employer now has the candidate thinking about personal achievement. A completed Quotient survey would not be a requirement for hire but rather an optional front-end tool in the company's hiring process.

This assessment covers a lot of ground for the hiring company. If the candidate is familiar with the Quotient, great. If not, the employer will be able to measure how nimble this candidate is at embracing a new process and getting the work done.

This is not too much for an employer to ask of a potential employee and not much of an additional burden for your hiring professionals. For those non-sales candidates who have never measured a personal accomplishment for value before, you will be able to observe how resourceful your candidate is when you receive their completed survey. Also, the information provided, robust or not so much, will make great fodder for the in-person interview.

An employer can also gauge an applicant's interest in the company by his or her willingness to complete this exercise. Some may find it difficult and bail. Better now than later, right? Experienced sales professionals should be able to knock this one out of the park.

WHAT MIGHT THIS ONLINE QUOTIENT SURVEY/PRIMER LOOK LIKE?

- It will offer up a brief overview of what the goal of the exercise is and how to complete it.

- It will clearly explain the QTNT PVC formula and provide at least one position-relevant example.

- It will ask the candidate to identify previous on-the-job accomplishments for his or her most recent places of employment. (The default option for each candidate will be the Q = 1, indicating they believe they delivered work on a level equal to their pay.)

- It will ask them to "show their work"—that is, how they determined the value of their contribution based on the QTNT formula: Value of Contribution ÷ Base Pay = QTNT score. There is no right or wrong way to do this.

- It will ask the candidate to explain how they were/are able to make or save money for their current or previous company and to indicate approximate amounts.

- It will prompt them to provide a QTNT score for each win and be prepared to defend their calculations. This will indicate the depth of their professional knowledge and, for the candidates' benefit, help prepare them for the in-person interview.

- It will ask them to provide peripheral information in support of their responses. This might include how they were able to deal with difficult personalities, employ creativity when seeking solutions, or demonstrate their ability to defuse problem situations before they got out of hand.

The hiring manager, being expert in the work to be performed and the specific skills required of the position, will be able to identify deception and any discrepancies found in responses, which will once again help narrow the candidate pool and speed up the process.

When the Quotient becomes an integral component of the accomplishments-based hiring process, our CEO, when asked how many people work for the company, should be able to say, "Nearly all of them."

44 A Very Brief Legal Look at the Quotient

I AM NOT AN attorney, and I have not consulted with any during the writing of this book. I have, however, spoken off the record with a few folks at the Equal Employment Opportunity Commission (EEOC) who informally concluded that I am on the right track with the Quotient, especially when it comes to fair pay.

LEGAL STANDING OF THE QUOTIENT

When it comes to the Quotient and equal pay for equal work, or, as you know I prefer, proper pay for the best performance, I believe the Quotient may have legal standing in a court of law as it relates to pay disparity issues. My humble opinion only.

As an example, I (a man) wind up the fiscal year with a QTNT score of 9, but my similarly qualified coworker, a woman, achieves a score of 17, nearly twice the contribution value that I delivered for the same period. But then I receive the promotion and the raise. Does the Quotient, in its achievement-based, defensible-calculation format, provide her with the necessary legal firepower to prevail? I think yes. Share this book with your corporate counsel and see what he or she thinks.

As I stated previously, your attorneys will embrace the Quotient when defending the organization against unlawful termination cases. The Quotient, then, might well become the first point of consideration for opposing counsel to consider before deciding to take on an unlawful termination or pay disparity case from the get-go.

45 Summing

WANT TO WRAP up *Leveling the Paying Field* by touching on those elements of the Quotient that are valuable to both the individual employee and the enterprise, no matter how large or small. But before doing so, I want my audience to understand that I know that the success of the Quotient *in application* will depend on the *motivated* individual—the person who will work the process as described in these pages to achieve pay parity and promotion. This is why, when publicly speaking on the Quotient, I never say that I have "solved" the pay disparity issue but rather that I have "resolved" the issue. I may be splitting hairs here, but it is important to say this: it will be the motivated individual who will pick up the ball and carry it across the goal line on their own.

That said, I am excited about the possibilities of utilizing the Quotient and the QTNT Personal Value Calculation/Contribution process as THE tool to overcome pay disparity issues. I recognize how big a statement this is, but I believe it will be proven to be accurate. It will take the combined action of workers and employers working in concert to achieve not only equal pay for equal work but also *proper pay for the best performance*. Proper pay for performance will add millions and billions to the purchasing power of those who gain from this effort. The economic impact alone is reason enough for businesses to embrace the Quotient.

Performance appraisal is tired. The only thing that has changed is the software—the fundamentals have not. Do they identify strengths and weaknesses? Well, I'm not sure. Ultimately, they remain subjective, and the immediate supervisor will almost always win "that argument." Again, just sayin'.

When implemented, the Quotient is an ideal employee engagement tool.

We can agree that we will never see all employees engaged at proposed/ projected/preferred/anticipated levels, but if an organization can get a significant number of employees thinking in terms of accomplishment and moving in the same direction, I think that will create a contagious attitude that will spread throughout the company.

The Quotient is an ideal tool for the targeting of potential candidates employed by the competition. A competitor can objectively estimate the potential, perhaps even the actual value, of these individuals to their company before determining if it's worth the time and effort to pursue them. Talk with your chief talent officer and recruiters about this idea.

So much time and money are spent in the screening-and-hiring process that businesses will welcome how the Quotient expedites the process. By implementing a "Quotient lite" pre-interview survey for potential candidates, companies will be able to quickly weed out those who are just shopping and not truly interested in making a change. This process also introduces your selected candidates to the Quotient and shows them what they can anticipate in formal interviews.

One of two unique aspects of the Quotient is in baselining performance expectations. The other is performance weighting to predetermine, if you will, what kind of work product is anticipated in return for an employee's pay package.

When it comes to pay for measurable performance, the Quotient works from both sides of the paycheck as a pay determinant. Rather than focusing only on equal pay for equal work, when the Quotient is properly implemented, both parties to the transaction will know why the employee is being paid what he or she is and what is expected of that employee in return (e.g., "A QTNT score of 7+ must be achieved before a bonus or options take effect"). In this way raises and bonuses are based on the active involvement of both parties in measurable achievement and verification.

Employees need to think of the Quotient as a mirror—a way of looking at themselves and clarifying their value to their company, to their industry, and to themselves. So many times I have told clients of all ages I believed they were aiming too low, and often that statement had a real impact when they realized I was right. The Quotient establishes value and is a goal-setting tool.

I hope to see the Quotient studied in business schools across the country. I know there are subsets of the C ÷ P formula to be modeled and exploited.

I don't know enough about artificial intelligence beyownd what I see, hear, and read in the media and online, but I believe the Quotient will have standing in the field of big data and will contribute to AI platforms today and into the future. The Quotient can be used in the measurement of global companies and industry verticals. There is a lot of data out there waiting to be mined and shared via the Quotient.

Lastly, the Quotient training curriculum is being developed even as I write this. Please visit RickGillis.com for QTNT performance valuation updates and to join the discussion. Thank you very much for taking the time to read and to learn how *Leveling the Paying Field* will positively impact both workers and employers now and into the future.—RG

APPENDIX I

A Pro's Take on Sourcing Accomplishments

Mike McRitchie (MikeMcRitchie.com) and I have been talking about job search, personal promotion, and, more recently, the Quotient for some time. He has adopted a few of my techniques, and I'm not afraid to borrow his—as you are about to see. What follows is Mike's very smart approach to identifying personal achievements.

TRIGGERS AND COOL STORIES

The biggest challenge people have is not a lack of accomplishments; they just haven't identified, quantified, and recorded them so they can be readily available when updating a résumé, professional profiles, or a presentation for promotion and performance appraisal. Generally, this is due to one of the following issues:

- **They don't recognize their accomplishments:** they aren't primed to recognize an accomplishment and appreciate its value to their brand and career.

- **They're not ready when it happens:** they accomplish something and then don't log it, so it's forgotten.

- **They overgeneralize:** they are not specific in the details of their accomplishments, which won't sell them as well as a clearly stated achievement will.

- **They don't craft a theme or a story:** You aren't just a job. You're not just a number. You are a unique person with unique skills, interests, abilities, and relationships that should all come together under an organizing theme or story. Similarly, each accomplishment can be viewed the same way. The key to this is thinking, "What is the moral of the story I'm telling with this accomplishment? What is the concept of the parable I'm telling?" Then, when you put all these stories together, you get a sense of who you are and what value you bring to your organization. It also helps you understand and better profile opportunities you should be targeting.

What I do: I help professionals dig into their past work history to *trigger defining accomplishments and cool stories* that will help them land their next career opportunity, whether that is within their current company or not. Then they use these marketing pieces to focus their efforts and communicate their value to their organization.

How I do my work: I start with the existing résumé. Here, I look at each job and try to figure out what the person has done and if there are any common themes I should explore with the client. Next, I schedule a one-hour call to discuss the details of the résumé and uncover accomplishments and stories. I ask my client these questions:

- What did you do in this role?
  - How did you do that?
  - How did it help the company?
  - Can you quantify that?
  - Tell me that story.
- What do you enjoy doing most?
- What do you think you're good at?
- What do you hear other people say you excel at?
- What are your three best qualities?
- What is most interesting about what you do now?
- What was your biggest challenge?

During this process, I take stream-of-consciousness notes. I don't critique or edit. I just get it all down as it comes out. I also ask follow-up questions on anything that seems interesting or is headed somewhere that might be valuable. Often I use a reporter's mentality to get the story. Ultimately, I look for one to three common themes or threads that I can fine-tune later.

I go through this exercise until I've got at least three solid stories, and ideally five. I then leverage those into eight to ten accomplishment bullets for Rick's Accomplishments Inventory. By going through this exercise, the results produce a more dimensional and interesting view of the client.

That's a lot to sort out, so let's look at each of these independently so you can see how they play a part in what will eventually be a solid Accomplishments Statement that performs for you.

YOU DON'T RECOGNIZE YOUR ACCOMPLISHMENTS.

This is an area most people struggle with. An accurate self-assessment can be difficult for people to determine on their own. You see yourself through the biases of your experience, or the current level of authority or power (given to you by the role or job title you have). You may over-estimate your skills and accomplishments. If you're the boss, getting the opinion of those you manage is not the best way to assess yourself. It may cause you to underestimate your skills. Or you may be so comfortable with your skills that you begin to assume they are common and not as valuable.

To get past this, you need outside assistance. Start with friends, family, or coworkers. You'll often find they can give you useful insights on what they consider your strengths or accomplishments. This is where working with a professional who can ask probing questions and help you uncover what is otherwise trapped in your memory is invaluable.

YOU'RE NOT READY TO CAPTURE ACCOMPLISHMENTS WHEN THEY HAPPEN

Imagine the feeling of bringing a big project in on time or under budget. Or you've delivered on your goals for a high-profile client. It feels good, right? That feeling might linger for a few days or weeks, but eventually you get busy. You're working on other projects or other initiatives, and you forget.

You find yourself at the end of the year preparing for your annual review. Maybe you're up for a promotion or a salary increase. You start to put together your review and . . . nothing. So, what happened? You can't recall what you did now that you need that information.

You can trigger your memory to capture great details. But if you don't somehow trigger your *detailed* memory properly, you either for-get it completely or it becomes a boring, blah storyline in your career—something without color, without details.

So what should you have done instead? Capture it. Get the details logged when they happen. There are a few ways to do this. Forward emails of accomplishments or acknowledgments from your boss, clients, or coworkers to a personal email address where you can collect them. Or save them into a file folder on your computer. Capture as much detail as possible. More is better. Share both the story details (what happened specifically) and the numbers (be very specific; don't round them off). You can always edit later. But remembering from scratch without any details in front of you is nearly impossible.

You can also dictate it to your smartphone. Tell the story in your own words, as if you're telling a friend. By doing this, it will also sound better and more like you. Then save the audio file with all your other accomplishments.

YOU OVERGENERALIZE YOUR ACCOMPLISHMENTS.

This inventory is more than just a list of past achievements and roles and responsibilities. Its purpose is to sell you to those who have the authority to promote you. It can't be boring. Often people are so focused on choosing the right words that they miss the resulting accomplishment.

You need to be specific. You need details. You need to convey a story (who you are, what you'll contribute to the team and the company). You need to do it in a meaningful, relevant, memorable way.

YOU DON'T ORGANIZE YOUR ACCOMPLISHMENTS INTO A CORE STORY.

Now put yourself in the reader's shoes. You are your manager. Review this document with fresh eyes. Scan quickly from top to bottom, twenty to thirty seconds max, just to get a sense of it.

In this thirty-second review, were you able to get a sense of who this person is, what he or she is about, and how this person's career has progressed? Can you recall an accomplishment or two? What stuck out in your mind? Are those things likely to impress management?

APPENDIX II

Sample Accomplishments Statement

Janet Best
Statement of Professional Accomplishments

- Delivered a 12% profit increase over prior regional management by establishing new institutional accounts resulting in $6,000,000 of new revenue. (Q 40)

- Completed special assignments on inventory phase-outs, unallocated materials, and obsolete inventory resulting in savings to the company of $1,500,000.   (Q 10)

- Improved operation scores for district to 90% from 82% in prior years as a result of group and individual coaching of district frontline employees. (Q 1)

- Successfully trained tristate team of over 800 managers, sales reps, technicians, and support staff on key company programs, which resulted in improving service levels by 10%, improved operations processes, and increased customer satisfaction.

- Managed direct reports of up to 40 associates, which included hiring, training, evaluating, coaching, and transitioning employees. Achieved a 34% decrease in turnover rate over previous management team.

- Repair center team ranked No. 1 in the country by J.D. Power & Associates. Achieved this level of customer satisfaction with the active involvement of all team members contributing to the plan.

- Improved past-due performance of vendors by implementing a daily expedite program. Result: Logistics performance improved 43% compared to past output; past-due orders reduced to 3% within 5 months.

- Led nation with an 18% improvement of sales in electronics by training store personnel on educating the customer on product functionality and reliability.

Glossary

=1: shorthand for a Quotient of one

>1: shorthand for a Quotient greater than one

<1: shorthand for a Quotient less than one

accomplishment: For Quotient purposes, an accomplishment is an achievement in the workplace that created anticipated or unanticipated revenue or saved money for the organization. An accomplishment can be achieved by an individual or accomplished by a team, branch, department, division, etc.

accomplishment format: A single-sentence format for stating the "what" and the "wow" of an employee's accomplishment using the following template: "Responsible for _____ that resulted in _____," where the first blank is filled in with *what* the speaker accomplished and the second blank represents the *value* of the accomplishment to the speaker's audience. Example: "Responsible for writing code that resulted in $12,000,000 in new client revenue."

accomplishments audit: the sourcing and compiling of a worker's notable career achievements.

Accomplishments Inventory™: The gathering of achievements; the compilation or listing of accomplishments used to identify the best and/or most valuable ones for presentation. See *accomplishments audit* and *Accomplishments Statement.*

accomplishments mindset: for Quotient purposes, another way for employees to think about and pay attention to on-the-job achievement, especially those achievements that are above and beyond what is required of their position.

Accomplishments Statement™: (1) A formal document listing an individual's personal best achievements on the job (see sample Accomplishments Statement, appendix II). (2) An individual statement found on the same document, or a single statement presented verbally by the person who performed the accomplishment.

aged out or aging out: For Quotient purposes, aging out is termination based on an employee's lack of performance when compared to their current rate of pay. Aging out specifically applies to the point in a person's career when they are producing less value for the organization than their rate of pay demands of them. Aging out should not be confused with age discrimination on the job. (See also *Earning Curve*.)

baseline: for Quotient purposes, a starting point for comparing employees within each vertical in an organization to determine their Quotient scores in the moment.

base pay: Take-home (net) pay plus other expenses attributed to you that are paid by your employer. These items include insurance, Social Security premiums, Medicare, payroll taxes, bonuses, company car, cell phone, training, etc.

Bureau of Labor Statistics (BLS): per BLS.gov, the US Department of Labor is the principal federal agency responsible for measuring labor market activity, working conditions, and price changes in the economy.

commercial value: For Quotient purposes, an employed worker has commercial value as determined by the market. Conditions affecting commercial value include the availability of jobs, the rate of pay, and the number of similarly qualified individuals available and willing to work in the same market. A worker demanding too high a rate of pay relative to their skills has little or no commercial value.

contractor: a person who accepts a position and is bound by a contract that identifies the work to be done and the time period in which said work should be completed.

Defensible Statement: For Quotient purposes, a statement made by an employee who does not have actual data or cannot precisely quantify the results of an achievement. This person will defend their statement's value with reasonable and conservative data so as not to overstate the value of the achievement. Defensible Statements should, by design, be factually conservative and not difficult to defend.

deliverables: a business- or project-management term for the quantifiable goods or services that will be provided (delivered) upon the completion of a project.

Earning Curve™: As developed by Rick Gillis, the Earning Curve is a graph that indicates that an employee's rate of production becomes less over time while their rate of pay continues to increase. When graphed, the rate of pay continues to rise while the rate of production, or earnings, curves downward.

fully loaded rate: A rate calculated by adding an hourly wage to fixed expenses. A fully loaded rate is a necessary consideration for anyone bidding project or contract work, so that they know their "loaded rate," or actual costs, prior to accepting a contract.

key performance indicators (KPI): A set of quantifiable measures that a company uses to gauge employee performance over time. KPIs are also used to determine a company's progress in achieving goals.

man-hour/person-hour/staff-hour: Refers to the amount of work an average person can accomplish in a single hour. This same definition can be applied to a day, a month, or a year.

nine-box grid (AKA nine-box talent matrix): Developed by McKinsey & Company in the 1960s, "nine box" is a widely known tool used in talent identification, succession planning, and employee development. The X axis, or horizontal line, of the grid indicates performance, while the vertical Y axis indicates leadership potential. An individual ranked in the lowest left corner is deemed a "nonperformer" or as being improperly utilized, while a person ranked in the upper right corner of the nine boxes is deemed to be a high-potential performer and probable future leader.

open-book management (OBM): a term coined by author John Case in 1993, OBM is the management style of providing all relevant financial information and critical data to line and staff employees so that better decisions can be made for the overall benefit of the enterprise.

project owner (AKA client or principal): an entity that enters into a contract with a contractor or vendor and receives specified goods and/or services under the terms of the work agreement.

PVC: An initialism for personal value calculation or contribution. See *QTNT PVC*.

Q1 or =1: A "perfect" QTNT score, which refers to a worker delivering exactly what was expected of them; a worker performing exactly the work they were hired to perform and no more. A reliably performing forklift driver could be an example of such an employee.

Q-Study™: A story of a worker's single professional accomplishment; the details involved in the sourcing/identifying of a person's work accomplishment to include the value of their contribution to the organization, which is then divided by their base pay to arrive at the resulting QTNT PVC rank or score. A Q-Study should be provided as background for each accomplishment presented during an employee's performance appraisal.

QTNT®: An acronym for, and pronounced as, "Quotient," QTNT describes the process, system, rank, formula, rating, or score used to determine a working person's value contribution to their employer. (2) The result of the Quotient calculation (C ÷ P = QTNT score) as utilized by the QTNT process and methodology.

QTNT calculation or formula: C ÷ P = QTNT where QTNT (representing the process of determining one's value on the job) equals the value of a worker's output in dollars (contribution, or C) divided by the amount of that worker's base pay (P) to produce the QTNT score, ranking, or rating.

QTNT exempt or QE: A position that does not meet the normal criteria of the QTNT and thus is not assigned a QTNT value. Example: A CEO's executive assistant who is paid significantly more than an administrative assistant due to intrinsic and incalculable considerations attributed to performance and the position.

QTNT PVC™: an abbreviation for the Quotient Personal Value Calculation process, or the Quotient Personal Value Contribution score, depending on context.

Rule of the Quotient: The larger the QTNT score, the larger and more valuable the contribution being delivered to the organization. An employee who scores a Quotient score of 30, assuming she is more or less equally qualified when compared to her coworker(s), is more valuable than one who scores a 9 during the same period. This definition also applies to teams, divisions, departments, etc. as well.

weight/weighting: For Quotient purposes, refers to all positions in an organization being "leveled" so that each employee is continuously seeking an =1 at minimum. (2) Weighting is a predetermination of the value of each position's required contribution for the overall success of the organization. Note that weighting refers to the position only and not the employee performing the work. Example: A delivery person may be weighted on a company scale as an =1 (pronounced "equal one"), which means that when he or she is making timely deliveries without incident, that person is performing up to the obligation of the established weight assigned that position. An engineer, on the other hand, may be weighted a 6, meaning that this individual is required/ expected to deliver value to the organization of six times their base pay to achieve an =1.

ACKNOWLEDGMENTS

The first person I must thank for her unconditional love and support is my wife, Mary. There is no way I could have accomplished all that I have over the last twenty-five years without her absolute belief in what I was doing.

There were several people I came to count on for their input and contribution to *Leveling the Paying Field*. In no particular order, I want to thank Kevin Martin, Cliff Bottoms, Wendy Schram, Doug Thorpe, Roger Ferguson, Greg Hohner, Catherine Bowers, Kim Buchsen, Jeff Wahl, Mike McRitchie, Joe Bontke, MyLin Lam, Diane Wilson, Gerry Crispin, Donna St.Onge Walls, Paul Freyre, Dale Quisenberry, Steve Carr, Anita Lauhoff, Barbara Lane, Scott Duncan, Terry Suffredini, John Case, Bill Fotsch, Anna Bassham, Peter Winick, Lane Transou, Jennifer Nahman, Andrea Nicholas and Greg Nicholas, Tanya Hall, Zeb LeVasseur, Erin Urban, Joey Liberty, Kevin Wisch, Richard Storey, Tracy Kearny, Tony Riedel, Jasmin Cattanach, Jill Silman-Chapman, Rod Branch, Will Vildibill, William Fitzgerald, Lisa Laumbach, Russell Tuncap, Elena Reznikova, Dave Able, Gargi Kundu, Sam Case, Alana Hill for her time and efforts in writing the Foreword, and my brother, Ron.

The people at Indigo River Publishing have been a professional joy to work with. Thank you, Dan Vega, Bobby Dunaway, Georgette Green and Dave Nathan for believing in *Leveling the Paying Field*. Thank you to Dianna Graveman and Regina Cornell for their extraordinary editing skills. Thank you, Emma Grace, for the terrific cover art and interior layout. I also want to thank Jackson Haynes for his editorial direction.

Thank you, all of you, for the time and "hand-holding" each of you provided to me in support of, and belief in, a little arithmetic formula I call QTNT PVC. I also want to thank friends and clients who allowed me to use their stories in the Q-Studies. Your names are lost to the ages—but then again, you might be listed above. (*Wink!*)

ABOUT THE AUTHOR

Rick Gillis was involved in the launch and success of the first two job boards in the greater Houston, Texas, area. Over a period of ten years of calling on professionals who hired others, Rick learned how job search actually worked. Paying attention to what hiring professionals wanted to see on a résumé and hear in an interview, and recognizing that what he was learning in their offices was not what he was seeing online or hearing at career events, Rick created his own highly successful, online-application-friendly, accomplishments-based résumé format, which he continues to recommend even today. It was at this time that he "invented" the white-out (keywords) technique,[6] which was very popular with job seekers in the Neolithically-early days of paper-résumé-filtering software.

This eventually led to his speaking across the US, appearing on as well as hosting radio and television shows in Houston, and being heard on radio and online in Australia, Panama, Canada, and the UK and across the Caribbean. Rick has been featured on NPR, PBS, and Business Insider and in the *Wall Street Journal, Forbes, Fortune, Inc.*, the *Houston Chronicle*, and *CIO*, to name just a few. Rick has also blogged for *CIO*, Salary.com, and *HuffPost Canada*.

Rick has written four books on job search and has worked with clients across the globe. *JOB! Search Optimized*, his most current self-published book on the topic, is available on Amazon. A fifth book, *PROMOTE!*, written for those professionals who aren't comfortable promoting themselves on the job, is the little book that begat the Quotient.

All of this, in concert with Rick's sales work and colorful personal life experience, has brought him to this place, to this book: *Leveling the Paying Field, A Groundbreaking Approach to Achieving Fair Pay*.

A graduate of Park University, Rick is also an artist and a musician. He lives with his wife, Mary, an attorney, and their passel of rescue pooches in the greater Houston area.

Rick is available for media, speaking, Quotient training, and consulting. Interested in writing a Quotient-based book for your industry or vertical? Contact Rick at linkedin.com/in/rickgillis. To engage in the QTNT discussion, visit RickGillis.com.

---

6   See next page

6   The "white-out technique" refers to the copying and pasting of an entire job posting at the bottom of a résumé, highlighting and reducing the font size to 1 pt., and then choosing "white" from the color palette to make the copy on the printed page "disappear." Use this tactic today and there is a good chance your résumé will be flagged by the software as deceitful and dismissed from consideration. Rick's current résumé format utilizes a visible keyword category at the bottom of the résumé that serves the same purpose. This better keyword-flagging technique can be found in his book, *JOB! Search Optimized.*

CPSIA information can be obtained
at www.ICGtesting.com
Printed in the USA
BVHW040017140422
634287BV00005B/147